UNANIMOUS PRAISE
FROM BOSSES ALL OVER AMERICA:

"I thought I was a monster before! This beautifully written book helped turn me into the 'Thing from Another World'!"
—R.L., AXLOTAL TELEGRAPH & TELEPHONE

"Now even my kids hate my guts! Especially the ones who work for me!" —C.W., CHEESEBOROUGH GUNS AND AMMO

"Broder showed me everyday, easy-to-use methods for torturing employees that would make Vlad the Impaler cringe!"
—P.N., CRAWLING EYE PRODUCTIONS

"I can now make them fear just getting out of bed in the morning, never mind actually showing up for a day's work! Bravo on all counts!" —L.L., SWEATSHOPPE SYSTEMS

AND EMPLOYEES PITIFULLY RESPOND:

"Why would you write such a book?"
—J.V., BILCHICK'S METAL FOUNDRY

"I went through thousands of hours of therapy to cope with my boss. Then she read your book! That's $45,000 down the drain!" —B.W., CONSOLIDATED CERAMICS OF COXSACKIE

"My boss loved your book—I'm writing this from the unemployment line. Thanks for nothing!"
—P.F., ANONYMOUS DOWNTRODDEN OFFICE WORKER

THE

BELOW-THE-BELT

MANAGER

ERIC BRODER

WARNER BOOKS

A Time Warner Company

Warner Books, Inc., 1271 Avenue of the Americas,
New York, NY 10020
Visit our Web site at http://warnerbooks.com
Ⓦ A Time Warner Company

First Printing: March 1998
10 9 8 7 6 5 4 3 2 1

Library of Congress Cataloging-in-Publication Data

Broder, Eric
    The below-the-belt manager / Eric Broder.
        p.   cm.
    ISBN 0-446-67310-2
        1. Management--Humor.   I. Title
PN6231.M2B76   1998

                                        97-34344
818' .5407--dc21   CIP

Cover design by Jon Valk
Cover illustration by Jeff Moores
Book design and composition by Fenix Design

FOR BOO ~~Teresa~~

Terry Bradshaw

ACKNOWLEDGMENTS

Many thanks to my agent, Loretta Barrett, Peggy Broder, Bill Gunlocke (the Cleveland writer's friend), Michael Heuer of Warner Books, my editor Rob McMahon, and Randy Siegel of the *Free Times*.

CONTENTS

INTRODUCTION: WHO AM I?

You can call me... *Sir.*

Why?

Because I'm the boss.

Me.

I'm the head honcho, the superchief, the commandant, the top dog, the chairman of the board.

Got it?

I'm in charge here. Nobody else. I'm running this pop stand. What I say goes. I'm the Man. It's my way or the highway. Do like I say or you're history. You mess with me, I'll be the last one you *ever* mess with. I'm *it.*

Get me?

I'm the chief executive officer of a successful company in the Midwest. I have a very high paying job. It wouldn't be polite to tell you exactly how much I earn in salary and bonuses, but believe me, it's much, *much* more than you.

I sit in a deluxe office, complete with wet bar, a Matisse and two Picassos on the walls, Corinthian leather furniture, a $15,000 stereo system, two secretaries, and a personal security guard. Adjacent to my office are a private gym, screening room, massage room, and a bathroom with a sunken whirlpool tub. I drive a Lexus and live in a $14 million home.

Why do I have all these nice things?

Because I get results. And getting results comes from knowing how to work with *people*.

Here is my definition of "people": *Creatures who do what I tell them to do, when I tell them to do it, while receiving as little pay from me as possible in return.* Yes, I treat employees the old-fashioned way: I exploit them.

I don't imagine that these people enjoy being underpaid, abused, ordered about without regard to their "feelings," and in general treated like faceless cogs in a huge, all-consuming machine.

But look at it from my point of view:

Who cares?

What is important is that *I* enjoy it, and that the company's bottom line enjoys it. The company's profits have increased 20 percent each year under my leadership. My board of directors sure likes those numbers. And they're not terribly interested in how I go about getting them, just as long as I do.

All this gives me a little thing we call absolute power.

The price for this power is that nobody really likes me. They call me a bastard. And that's when they're feeling charitable.

Let me show you how you can be a bastard, too.

I wrote this book because quite a few management and leadership books have crossed my desk in the past several years. These books use a variety of words in their titles and in chapter headings that keep popping up again and again. Words like "empowerment," "reengineering," "nurturing," "praise," "learning," "communication," "healing," "listening," "teamwork," "balance," "rewards," "Tao," "dignity," and "heart."

You won't find these words in this book. I'm going to kill these words.

Here *are* a few of the words you'll find in my book:

PAIN	FEAR	PUNISHMENT
DISCIPLINE	INTIMIDATION	OPPRESSION
DOWNSIZING	THREATEN	BLAME
LACKEY	UNDERLING	FUNCTIONARY
PUNK	NITWIT	NUMSKULL

FIRE (AND ITS COUSINS DISMISS, DISCHARGE, CAN, BOOT, PINK-SLIP, SACK, TERMINATE, ETC.)

SCAPEGOAT (NOUN AND VERB FORMS)

If you love these words as much as I do—if they make you tingle all over—then you've got what it takes to learn the qualities of *genuine* leadership. And you should read on.

If you *don't* love these words—if they "shock" you, or make you all whiny and weepy—then by all means read those other touchy-feely management books I mentioned earlier. You and all your little friends can "reward" and "nurture" yourselves right out of your jobs.

The rest of us will run things.

Just stay the hell out of our way.

THE EXECUTIVE TEST

Here is a little multiple-choice test I'd like you to take to see what aptitude you have—if any—to become *my* kind of leader.

Answer these questions truthfully. You might as well know right now if you're cut out to be a high-powered hard-driving executive, or just some wriggling lackey who is doomed to receive it in the rear forever.

(1) A CLERK SAYS "GOOD MORNING" AND PATS YOU ON THE SHOULDER. YOU SHOULD:

    A. Say "Good morning" back

    B. Smile and pat the clerk's hand

    C. Wink and give a thumbs-up

    D. Cringe and insert the impertinent scumbag at the very tippy-top of your shitlist

(2) AN EMPLOYEE HELPS YOU FIX A FLAT ON THE FREEWAY. YOU SHOULD:

    A. Thank the employee effusively on site

    B. Send a thank-you note to the employee's home

    C. Have Security run a thorough check on the employee. Sooner or later this so-called Good Samaritan will be looking for payback, and you'll want to find every bit of dirt you can on this bastard who's ready, willing, and able to suck the blood clean out of you…and make no mistake, you'll be sucked down to the bone

(3) AN EMPLOYEE CONFRONTS YOU WITH THE FACT THAT SEVERAL MONTHS AGO, IN A WEAK MOMENT, YOU HAD PROMISED A PROMOTION AND RAISE IN SALARY. YOU SHOULD:

    A. Immediately follow through on your promise

    B. Say you can't recall any such promise and apologize profusely

    C. Promise to review the request and get back to him or her

    D. Spike the smart-ass's urine with cocaine and pop a surprise drug test

(4) AN EMPLOYEE IS CAUGHT EMBEZZLING FROM YOUR COMPANY. YOU SHOULD:

A. Fire the employee immediately and prosecute

B. Fire the employee immediately but do not prosecute

C. Thank your lucky stars that now you have the perfect "blackmailable" chump who will indulge your every whim, whether it falls into the category of simple dirty tricks or third-degree felony

(5) A FEMALE EMPLOYEE INFORMS YOU THAT SHE IS PREGNANT. YOUR RESPONSE?

A. "Oh, how marvelous! Congratulations!"

B. "Yeah, well here's a news bulletin for you: I'm not about to let this company go into the crapper just because an irresponsible tart goes out and gets herself knocked up."

C. "Oh, that's wonderful! Congratulations!"

(6) YOUR PRIMARY FUNCTION AS A LEADER IS TO ENSURE:

A. Misery

B. Punishment

C. Discipline

D. Terror

E. All of the above

(7) AN EMPLOYEE CONSISTENTLY COMES UP WITH AN AMAZING NUMBER OF GOOD, WORKABLE IDEAS FOR YOUR COMPANY. YOU SHOULD:

A. Encourage the employee and create a nurturing environment where he or she can continue to flower

B. Put the employee on a fast track within your organization

C. Publicly give credit to the employee for all of her or his ideas

D. Use the ideas, claim them as your own, then deposit the smarty-pants on the first bus out of town

(8) SECRET LAVATORY TAPES REVEAL THAT UNDERLINGS ARE SPEAKING DISRESPECTFULLY OF YOU. YOU SHOULD:

    A. Swallow hard and consider carefully whether or not their criticisms are warranted

    B. Do nothing and immediately remove any and all recording mechanisms from your company's lavatories. What were you thinking?

    C. Pointedly repeat some of the phrases they used to their faces and watch them bleed out their ears

(9) YOU SHOULD NEVER DISCOURAGE EMPLOYEES WHEN YOU CAN JUST AS EASILY:

    A. Encourage them

    B. Support them

    C. Lend them a helping hand

    D. Dash their hopes and dreams against the rocks of despair

(10) FEEDBACK FROM EMPLOYEES IS:

    A. Crucially important

    B. The heartbeat of any organization

    C. A welcome sign that they're involved

    D. A pain in the ass

(11) THE BEST PLACE TO CRITICIZE AN EMPLOYEE IS:

    A. Privately, in your office

    B. Privately, but in an informal setting, perhaps at lunch

    C. Loudly and publicly for optimal humiliation

(12) AN EMPLOYEE SAYS HE OR SHE DESPERATELY NEEDS SOME TIME OFF FOR PERSONAL REASONS. YOUR RESPONSE?

    A. "Certainly, but keep us informed of what's going on."

    B. "Absolutely, but be sure to give Personnel an idea of when you expect to be back."

    C. "Of course—I hope everything will be okay. Don't worry about the details, we'll work them out later. You just go on and do what you have to do. Best of luck."

D. "You walk out of here now, you lose the address of this
building permanently, *capeesh?* You walk out now, you walk
out for good."

**(13) A GOOD WAY TO KEEP EMPLOYEES' MORALE AT A HIGH
LEVEL IS:**

A. To take your team out to lunch every few weeks
B. To give surprise bonuses when morale seems to be dipping
C. To single out individuals each month for stellar performances
D. None of your concern

**(14) YOU CATCH AN EMPLOYEE EATING AN UNAUTHORIZED
TREAT SUCH AS A HOSTESS TWINKIE AT HIS OR HER DESK.
WHAT DO YOU DO?**

A. Ask the employee to finish the treat in the lunchroom
B. Circulate a memo requesting that employees not eat treats at
their desks
C. Take the offending treat out of the employee's hand, squeeze
it until the cream oozes out between your fingers, toss the
flattened and crushed item on the employee's desk, wipe
your hand on the employee's shirt or blouse, and whisper,
"How do you like your Twinkie now, my friend?...*How do
you like your Twinkie now?*"

**(15) AN UNFLATTERING DRAWING OF YOU WITH THE LEGEND
"ASSHOLE OF THE CENTURY" INSCRIBED BENEATH IT CIR-
CULATES THROUGH THE OFFICE. YOU SHOULD:**

A. Ignore it
B. Take a good hard look at yourself—perhaps you'll ascertain
why such a drawing would be rendered
C. Draw a picture of a little dog next to the figure to show
what a good sport you are
D. Make good-and-goddamn sure you live up to the title

**(16) AN ENTHUSIASTIC JUNIOR MANAGER PUTS UP A
"SUGGESTION BOX" IN THE OFFICE. YOU SHOULD:**

A. Read any and all suggestions and keep an open mind

B. Have periodic meetings to discuss the suggestions you find
most stimulating and provocative

C. Put a sign on the box saying: "Here's a suggestion for those
planning to put suggestions in the Suggestion Box: *You can
be replaced.*"

**(17) AN EMPLOYEE COMES UP TO YOU TO PERSONALLY INVITE
YOU TO HIS OR HER HOME FOR A DINNER PARTY. YOU
SHOULD:**

A. Politely decline, and thank him or her for the invitation

B. Graciously accept and make a point of it to attend, for at
least a short while

C. Laugh in his or her face and say, "Oh, right! Do you want
me to bring the malt liquor and barbecue potato chips or
will you be supplying those?…Get a clue, you insolent half-
wit."

**(18) IN A LETTER OF REFERENCE FOR A WORKER WHO CHOOSES
TO LEAVE YOUR EMPLOY, YOU SHOULD CLOSE WITH "I AM
SURE THAT (HE/SHE) WILL NOT:**

A. "fail to do a fine job for you."

B. "disappoint you."

C. "let minor obsessions with hallucinogenic drugs and
bondage interfere with the job at hand."

**(19) YOU RUN INTO AN EMPLOYEE AT A RESTAURANT.
YOU SHOULD:**

A. Say hello and chat briefly

B. Ask him or her to join your party

C. Brush past the parasite as if he or she didn't exist

(20) **A GROUP OF YOUR MANAGERS COMES TO YOU AND ASKS THAT YOU MEET WITH THEM TO DISCUSS IMPROVEMENTS TO YOUR COMPANY'S BENEFITS PACKAGE. YOU:**
- A. Set up a meeting immediately
- B. Go to each manager and get individual input
- C. Be sure to do your own extensive research into the matter before you meet with them
- D. Wiggle off the hook as you always do

(21) **A PROMINENT MEMBER OF THE LOCAL MEDIA CALLS TO GET YOUR RESPONSE TO VARIOUS ACCUSATIONS MADE PUB-LICLY BY DISGRUNTLED EX-EMPLOYEES. YOU SHOULD SAY:**
- A. Absolutely nothing, and instruct your PR professional to prepare a release in reference to any and all charges
- B. "No comment at this time."
- C. "Now, do I seem to you like I run that kind of compa-ny?...Come on into the office, and let's talk about how we can make you happy. Because I know you like nice things. Am I right?"

(22) **THE EXPRESSION ON YOUR FACE AS YOU WALK THROUGH THE OFFICE SHOULD REFLECT A PERSONALITY THAT MIGHT BEST BE DESCRIBED AS:**
- A. Commanding
- B. Confident
- C. Serene
- D. Sociopathic

(23) **AN EMPLOYEE EMOTIONALLY INFORMS YOU THAT HIS OR HER SALARY ISN'T ENOUGH TO MAKE ENDS MEET, BUT THE EMPLOYEE'S PERFORMANCE DOESN'T MERIT AN INCREASE. YOU SHOULD SAY:**
- A. "I'm terribly sorry, but the budget doesn't permit us to increase your salary at this time."
- B. "I'm sorry to hear about your troubles, but, to be frank, your performance lately simply doesn't warrant a raise in pay.

Come back in six months and we'll discuss it again."
C. "Go to hell."

(24) THE ORGANIZATION OF YOUR OFFICE SHOULD MOST RESEMBLE:
A. A family tree
B. A horizontal grid
C. An ant farm

(25) THE ATMOSPHERE OF YOUR OFFICE SHOULD MOST RESEMBLE:
A. A university classroom
B. A think tank
C. Death row

(26) WHEN YOUR EMPLOYEES THINK OF YOU, THEY SHOULD MOST CLOSELY ASSOCIATE YOU WITH WHICH NOTABLE PERSONALITY?
A. Eleanor Roosevelt
B. Mahatma Gandhi
C. Dr. Martin Luther King, Jr.
D. Abraham Lincoln
E. Mother Teresa
F. Hannibal Lecter

(27) WHEN YOU ARE FORCED TO FIRE AN EMPLOYEE WHO NEVER FIT IN YOUR COMPANY, YOU SHOULD:
A. Do it face to face
B. Remain impassive as you do it
C. Do it with compassion and generosity of spirit
D. Candidly explain and categorize all the reasons for the dismissal
E. Say, "It's my distinct pleasure to inform you that you're history. You don't exist anymore. You never happened. Now get your ass out that door....By the way, I hate your goddamn clothes."

(28) IN YOUR IN-HOUSE NEWSLETTER, MAKE CERTAIN THAT ANY OF YOUR WRITTEN MESSAGES TO EMPLOYEES CONTAIN THESE WORDS, OR SOMETHING SIMILAR:

A. "We continue to make steady progress toward our goals."

B. "As always, you should feel free to come see me with any suggestions or concerns you might have."

C. "We're looking forward to the most exciting times ever here....I know we're all up to the challenges ahead."

D. "Attention, workers of my employ: The unfortunate fate of _____, while regrettable, may serve as a useful object lesson to you all: You mind your p's and q's, and you won't get hurt.

"I'm not paying you to read newsletters. Get back to work."

(29) IN A MIRROR, YOU CATCH AN EMPLOYEE PANTOMIMING TAKING AIM AT THE BACK OF YOUR HEAD WITH AN IMAGINARY RIFLE. YOU SHOULD:

A. Good-naturedly pretend to be hit

B. Turn around and shake your head sadly at this foolishness

C. Spin, pull out your own not-imaginary-one-bit weapon, and do the old Dirty Harry routine of wondering aloud just how many bullets are left in the cylinder: "Do you feel lucky, punk? *Well, do you?*"

(30) SEVERAL OF YOUR EMPLOYEES HAVE BEEN GROUPED AROUND THE WATERCOOLER CHATTING FOR A LONGER PERIOD OF TIME THAN YOU'D LIKE. YOU SHOULD:

A. Join them—they'll break up soon enough

B. Stand nearby, raising an eyebrow to suggest that perhaps it's time to disperse

C. Release the hounds

(31) BECAUSE OF SETBACKS, YOU HAVE BEEN FORCED TO MAKE MOVES THAT MAY EVENTUALLY HAVE A NEGATIVE IMPACT ON MANY OF YOUR EMPLOYEES' PAYCHECKS. YOU SHOULD:

A. Circulate a memo throughout your organization explaining step by step what happened and why

B. Be up-front about what happened, taking complete responsibility

C. Make certain that everyone knows you're taking as big a hit as they are

D. Triple the presence of Security in the office—these people are animals

Answer key:	1. D	2. C	3. D	4. C	5. B	6. E	7. D
	8. C	9. D	10. D	11. C	12. D	13. D	14. D	15. D
	16. C	17. C	18. C	19. C	20. D	21. C	22. D	23. C
	24. C	25. C	26. F	27. E	28. D	29. C	30. C	31. D

If you answered fewer than twenty-five of these questions correctly, you ought to think twice about your career choice. The curve may seem extreme to you, but any mistakes will assuredly translate into chinks in your armor—and if your employees detect these chinks, they'll be all over you like stink on a monkey. Before you know it, the inmates will be running the asylum.

However, if you want to get a *perfect* score on this test, read on. If you've got the guts.

NOW YOU'RE IN CHARGE

Let's begin by assuming you have reached the conclusion of your journey to the top. This book isn't about getting there; it's about *being* there—and, more important, *staying* there.

Before I start, I do realize that many of you may be curious as to exactly how I worked my way up to head this organization.

Unfortunately, my attorneys have advised me that because so many cases relating to this subject are still under litigation, I am not permitted to speak directly about them.

But I would like to briefly say a few words to some disgruntled former employees of this company, who know who they are.

You people are throwing around a lot of fancy words about me. Liar. Weasel. Fraud. Ass kisser. Double-crosser. Predator. Sociopath. Psychotic.

You talk about things like back-stabbing and double-dealing. Blackmail. Extortion. Harassment. Campaigns of dirty tricks and character assassination. You say I ought to be put away where decent people can't see me. Well!

If I didn't know better, I'd say I detect the faint odor of *sour grapes* here.

Why don't you people give it up? By the time the courts get this all sorted out we'll all be long in our graves. Are you going to spend the rest of your lives pursuing this?

Because if you are, I warn you: I am going to bury you. You'll be lucky to find jobs selling discount size-AAAAA shoes. You'll be eating *tuna sandwiches* for dinner, my friends! And I'm not talking fancy albacore, I'm talking chunk light! *House* brand! *If* you're lucky! Just who do you think you're dealing with here? Mother-freaking *Teresa*?

Let's move beyond the pitiful squeaks of the little people— and on to the massive roars of the big ones.

WHAT KIND OF LEADER ARE YOU RIGHT NOW?

So we're assuming you have completed your journey to the top, right into the big corner office. You are now the executive of executives. You're the main ingredient, you're the straw that stirs the drink.

You're the capo di tutti capi (the Boss of All Bosses).

Excellent. But just what kind of boss are you?

Are you...

A Whiner?

A Beggar?

A Wimp?

If you're part of the vast majority of leadership out there, chances are you're one of the three.

It's no surprise. You've been duped by all this "compassionate" and "caring" management hogwash into believing that's the way you *should* be. I'm here to tell you that caring and compassion is for nurses, nuns, and schoolteachers.

Come on...you're *better* than that!

Here is a brief look at how these types think:

• *The Whiner:* "Jeez, I didn't hire these people to just sit around. They're taking advantage of me, but if I say anything they'll think I'm criticizing them and not respecting their dignity. Jeez, this is really frustrating."

• *The Beggar:* "*Please* do your job, I'd really be grateful, oh, whenever, oh, that'd be great, oh, thanks so much."

• *The Wimp:* "I'll just ask Hopkins to order these people to get moving on this project. I'll go back in my office and pretend to be on the phone just in case they come in and complain about him and maybe in the meantime the work'll get done."

Disgusting, isn't it? Is that the kind of leader you want to be?

If it is, I suggest you go out and buy one of those caring, compassionate, nurturing, etc., management books. Sooner than you think, you'll be able to read it aloud to all the other Whiners, Beggars, and Wimps in your Unemployed Executive Support Group and you can drink your little cups of herbal tea together and have a good cry.

If you want to be *my* kind of leader—if you want to make people jump, wrap'em around your finger, make'em dance to your tune, tote that barge, lift that bale, do it 'til you're satisfied, and so on and so forth—then you have to let them know who's boss from the get-go.

To find out how, read on.

You're Not One of "Them"
Anymore—Thank God

The fact is, now that you're no longer part of the low-grade, common muck, you really can't afford to be human anymore. Just wave bye-bye to that portion of your personality right now, and say good riddance.

It should please you to know that being inhuman is really not that difficult. It's amazing how quickly you can get the hang of it. Between you and me? *Being inhuman is one hell of a good time.*

Let's talk about your appearance, attitude, and bearing, to get you to that nonhuman place you want to be.

The Executive Appearance

It all begins with your physical appearance. Now that you're different, you have to *look* different.

(*Note:* Be sure to have your attorneys insert a clause in your contract specifying that your company will pay for these clothes, surgeries, medical procedures, etc.)

• *Outfit yourself in the finest, most expensive designer suits.* Make sure they are tailored to perfection. Matching silk shirts and ties, and the best Italian shoes, spit-shined to reflective power (you may appoint a specified shoe-shining lackey to help you achieve this effect). Your clothing must make your inferiors understand that your wardrobe is not only out of their league but out of their universe. You want them to believe that even *thinking* about a suit like yours costs. This is a critical first step on your power trip.

(True story: When I wore my Armani to the mall one day, some hippie came up to me and told me in disgust, "Do you know an entire Third World family could eat for six months on what you paid for that suit?" Imagine the spring that put in my step!)

• *Your hair must be close-cropped.* Crew cut, buzz cut, Pat Riley slick-back, whatever. As long as it hugs the skull, and not a follicle out of place. If you are bald, go all the way with it and shave your head. (Pince-nez? If you like. The Prussian look, though not absolutely necessary, is always a winner. If you go the Prussian route, don't forget the riding crop—the accessory that doubles as a threat.)

Ladies, if your hair looks soft, then so will you. Spray it until it looks like it could chip off your head. Or wear a Nancy Reagan or Margaret Thatcher wig. Your hair should make Zsa Zsa Gabor's look totally natural and organic.

• *Keep your clothing immaculately clean.* Food remnants on your tie, blouse, shirt, pants, or skirt are an absolute no-no. These people should not suspect that you need to eat. Lead them to believe you are a self-sufficient being, that you can feed yourself for weeks on food stored within your body. Impressive—and scary, too.

• *Never wear a cologne or perfume.* You must be essentially odorless. Does a rock smell? Does steel? If you want to be as hard as these things, you have to smell like them. By which I mean not at all.

• *If you have a propensity to sweat, lose it.* You should be as dry as a bone. But you should not look like you *contain* bones within you. You should look like a piece of solid matter, a cyborg. (My doctor gives me weekly injections that make my skin as hard as an industrial-strength polymer. If you press my skin with your finger, you will find total resistance.)

• *You should not look like you need air.* Wimps need air. If you must appear to breathe, do so in the privacy of your office. You don't want to show these people *any* vulnerability.

• *Your mouth should be no more than a slit.* You know how some Hollywood stars make their lips fuller through collagen injections? You need to do the exact opposite: surgically remove any excess lip flesh that could indicate softness or weakness. Rent the movie *The Sound of Music* (I know, I know—but this is purely for research) and look at Christopher Plummer's mouth. That mouth—a thin, cruel slash—contains the lips of a true executive. Go for it.

• *Your eyes should be totally lifeless.* Rent the movie *Jaws* and look at Bruce the shark's eyes. Study the scene in which Bruce chomps down on Robert Shaw like a crunchy dill. That's exactly the way you want your eyes to look when you're chomping down on an underling. (Sometimes I wear special pupil-and-iris-obscuring contact lenses that make my eyes completely white when I particularly want to intimidate someone. Very effective.) Your eyes are supposedly the windows to your soul. As you don't have a soul, your eyes need to reflect that.

All of which leads us into the subject of establishing your executive demeanor—the face you present to underlings day after day.

Just remember: The word doesn't have "demean" in it for nothing.

THE EXECUTIVE DEMEANOR

An executive demeanor is a serious one—*dead* serious. If your executive board wanted a smiley, giggly, laughing leader, they would have chosen Jimmy Carter or Pee-Wee Herman. They certainly didn't choose Jimmy Carter or Pee-Wee Herman. They chose you.

Therefore, your demeanor must project the very essence of your leadership.

Here are the Crucial Truths of your leadership that your facial expression needs to impart at all times to underlings:

1. I AM IN CHARGE.

2. I AM ABOVE YOU.

3. YOU ARE NOT THE LOW PERSON ON THE TOTEM POLE.
   YOU ARE <u>UNDER</u> THE TOTEM POLE.

4. YOU ARE A PEON.

5. YOU HAVE ZERO POWER.

6. YOU COULD BE REPLACED BY ALMOST ANY MAMMAL.

7. I AM IN CHARGE.

8. I AM ABOVE YOU, ETC., ETC.

Repeat these Truths to yourself as you walk around your office, and your countenance will eventually reflect them. Mix this (richly deserved) haughtiness with your semi-human physical presence and, believe me, you will be one intimidating presence. A presence at once forbidding yet terrifying. It is your Total Executive Demeanor.

Remember that your own days of gazing worshipfully and adoringly at your superiors and kissing ass to win favor are long gone. Now the shoe is on the other foot—*your* foot. Now it's time for *kicking* ass, not kissing it.

All right. You've got the look.

How do you put it into action?

RELATING TO INFERIORS DAY TO DAY

You are a higher species. It's time for you to act like one.

Let's take a look at some concrete examples on the direction you must take in relating to the common clay.

• *When an underling says something inconsequential to you such as "Good morning," never, ever respond by saying "Good morning."* Replying in this manner elevates common, salaried employees to your level. It's a sure sign of weakness and, ultimately, vulnerability. (If you happen to say "Good morning" and add the inferior's name—well, you might as well hand over the keys to your office right there. If you give these people one inch of humanity, they'll take a mile.)

Here are a few approaches to the "Good morning" question that you may take:

Reply with something ambiguous—and thus chilling. This tactic is extremely handy with employees you know little or nothing about.

> UNDERLING: Good morning, sir.
> YOU: For some, perhaps. For you? Who knows.

With others, it may be better to take a more directly assertive approach:

> UNDERLING: Good morning, sir.
> YOU: I am in charge here. Make no mistake about it. *I am in charge here.*
> UNDERLING: Yes, sir.

Or the curtly dismissive attitude, which is helpful in making others feel small:

> UNDERLING: Good morning, sir.
> YOU (*pushing employee aside*): If you have something to say to me, get it in writing.

To get a certain message across to a known miscreant, use the small-town police officer approach:

> UNDERLING: Good morning, sir.
> YOU: Now what in *hell* you mean by that? Huh?
> UNDERLING (*quickly*): Nothing, nothing.
> YOU: You best keep your mouth shut, and your nose clean. You sass me again and I'll leave you every way but alone. You hear me?
> UNDERLING: Yes, sir.

YOU: What's that? I can't hear you!
UNDERLING: *Yes, sir!*

My personal favorite, however, is to employ a cold silence accompanied by a sneer and a flinch. Both strongly indicate my displeasure at the disruption of my personal physical and aural space.

Any of the above will get you off to a winning start in the morning—and set the tone for the rest of the day. Use these same conversational gambits anytime an inferior attempts to exchange pleasantries with you. Whenever anyone says "Hello" or "How are you" or "Nice to see you," you can be sure of two things: *They want what you've got,* and *they'll shamelessly suck up to get it.*

Don't let 'em. Cut 'em off at the knees.

Here are some other keys:

• *Never directly look at underlings when they are talking to you.* Look beyond them, off into the distance, as they speak. And check your wristwatch often. This lets them know that they are *wasting your time.*

• *Vital: You* must *master the art of looking down on people, even if you are not physically able to do so.* Practice in front of a mirror at home by placing a mark several inches above your head and sneering at it. Remember: Never look directly at the mark—keep telling yourself that all it is is a poorly paid functionary. A peon. A peasant. The smallest of the small. And you are the largest of the large.

• *Explosiveness at the proper time—by which I mean an entirely unexpected time—keeps underlings on their toes.* Tossing in some psychotic language may also be helpful. Nobody argues with a lunatic.

For example:

UNDERLING: In the second quarter, our plan to move quickly ahead on the Web site project should be on target, and our goal to—

YOU: Move quickly ahead? Do you call what you have written down here *moving quickly ahead*? I've known turtles who've moved faster than this! Snails! Chickens! Goats! You people are "moving quickly ahead," all right— to the unemployment line! I'll fire you all! I'll fire the *world*, dammit!

You may not mean any of this—at the moment. But they don't know that. Remember, a little dementia goes a long way.

GOLDEN RULE: Always, always, *always* move away from an underling *before* he or she is finished talking with you, preferably in midsentence. This discomfiting device is yet another way to let them know you can barely tolerate their unfortunately necessary presence in your organization.

A REAL-LIFE CONVERSATION WITH A FUNCTIONARY

The following is a transcript of a recent conversation I secretly taped with a low-level employee—a conversation that demonstrates perfectly what I've been talking about.

This functionary, judging from everything he said, was clearly out to sandbag and eventually replace me, as they all are. We'll call him Smith.

SMITH: Good morning, sir. It's a very nice morning.

ME: Is it? We'll see about that.

SMITH: Yes, it's absolutely beautiful out. The sun's shining, there's low humidity—

ME: Is this a weather report? Would you *rather* be outside? I can arrange that—permanently. You want to live in a cardboard box outside? I can arrange that.

SMITH: Yes, sir. Sir, I wanted to talk to you about an idea I had concerning organizing the production area to make—

ME: Because I don't have time to listen to weather reports all day. I have a business to run.

SMITH: Yes, sir, and I think I can help it run—

ME: Are you interrupting me? If you're interrupting me there'll be hell to pay.

SMITH: No, sir, I'm not. I just wanted to say I had an idea to organize the production area to better facilitate the—

ME (*moving away*): Watch your step, I'm warning you.

End of conversation. Did you see how I thwarted Smith's shameless, grasping ambition? Did you see how Smith was trying to suck up, get on my good side, and ooze his way into my confidence, thus positioning himself perfectly to then deposit a dagger in my back and take over?

Sorry, Smith. I'm way ahead of you. On your knees, dog.

Here's another bonus: From now on Smith is one smarty-pants who'll keep his ideas to himself. I put up a wall he'll never attempt to scale again. You must make your Executive Wall as impenetrable as mine—unless you *want* people and ideas to find their way through. Unless you *want* the whole structure to come crashing down around you.

So you make that Wall as high as you can, and you put some barbed wire at the top. And if you're smart you'll electrify it—so anyone who tries something cute will get the shock of his or her life.

TEN THINGS TO REMEMBER NOW THAT YOU'RE THE BOSS

1. NEVER FORGET THAT YOU ARE IN CHARGE BECAUSE YOU ARE BETTER THAN EVERYONE ELSE. FAR BETTER. IT'S NOT EVEN CLOSE.

2. YOUR IDEAS ARE BRILLIANT. THEIR IDEAS ARE CRETINOUS. ON THOSE OCCASIONS WHEN THEIR IDEAS AREN'T CRETINOUS, TAKE THEM OVER AND MAKE THEM YOUR OWN.

3. EMPLOYEES ARE PEONS. TREAT THEM ACCORDINGLY.

4. IF YOU'RE FEELING DOWN, GIVE YOURSELF A BOOST BY TELLING YOURSELF, "I CAN FIRE SOMEONE TODAY."

5. EVERY EMPLOYEE WANTS TO SEE YOU DEAD. TREAT THEM ACCORDINGLY.

6. PATIENCE WITH OTHERS IS FOR SCHMUCKS.

7. PEASANTRY CAN BE INFECTIOUS. KEEP AWAY FROM YOUR LOW-LEVEL EMPLOYEES AS MUCH AS POSSIBLE.

8. KEEP YOUR NOSE IN THE AIR. TRY TO LOOK AS IF YOU'RE SMELLING SOMETHING FOUL.

9. IF YOU EXPOSE ANY VULNERABILITY, THESE PEOPLE WILL BE AT YOU LIKE PIRANHA UNTIL THERE'S NOTHING LEFT OF YOU BUT YOUR FIVE-THOUSAND-DOLLAR SUIT AND CROCODILE-SKIN SHOES LEFT IN A SMALL PILE ON THE FLOOR.

10. YOU ARE ALL-POWERFUL, THE MOST FABULOUS, THE GREATEST OF THE GREAT. IF ANYONE TRIES TO TELL YOU DIFFERENT, GET RID OF THEM.

KEEPING YOURSELF ON TOP

THE BASIC HIERARCHY

I've been hearing that the vertical hierarchy within organizations is becoming obsolete and is gradually being replaced by the *horizontal* hierarchy. That "enlightened" companies are now encouraging self-managed teams and collaboration among workers of every stripe. Grunts performing management duties; management performing grunt duties. People working together toward a common goal. People as equals. People being *empowered.*

Sound familiar?

Perhaps you recognize this as a philosophy a certain bearded loony toon named Marx—and I sure don't mean Groucho—first espoused many years ago. Do you recall what that philosophy is?

That's correct. It's called *communism.* Where all share equally in all things, and where labor is organized for common advantage. Now it's being preached for American business!

Before you know it we'll all be wearing woolen jumpsuits and sandals, holding hands and singing incomprehensible folk songs. Then we'll all go back to our collectives to sleep on mats. And we'll be plenty tired, because we'll have spent the day waiting in line to get a pork ear from the People's Butcher. But that's communism for you.

Well, what the hell—it was a big hit in Russia, right?

Don't waste your time with this crap. Far from becoming a horizontal hierarchy, your business needs to verticalize even more.

I'm not talking about the classic organizational pyramid, with various senior managers creeping up that incline toward you and your Executive Suite. I'm talking a ninety-degree drop here, from the top—you—to the bottom. The bottom being everyone but you (see illustration).

YOUR EXECUTIVE HIERARCHY

YOU, THE MAGNIFICENCE

AIR | AIR

PEONS, FUNCTIONARIES, SUBJECTS, ETC.

What you want is you at the very tippy-top, all by yourself. And all others—from your top senior management to the lowliest dolt who empties the wastebaskets—scrambling for position below. You have to make sure *their* position is always far, far away from you. You don't want anyone within even shouting distance.

I can hear you say: "But it's *lonely* up there."

I say: "There's *absolute power* up there." And believe me, absolute power beats the snot out of loneliness every time.

KEEPING POWER WHERE IT BELONGS

There are various strategies you can use to maintain that iron grip on your power. But the best way to keep power *with* you is to keep it *from* others.

Keeping Power from Your Closest Competitors

Let's talk about keeping power away from your most dangerous potential rivals: those directly under you. After all, they've climbed the ladder, put in their years, and many of them aim to ultimately succeed you.

Some of you might be saying, "Well, that's the natural progression of things. People succeed people in jobs—even the top jobs."

Well, I say: Fat chance. Ain't nobody succeeding nobody.

Did you work this hard and this long for that? Did you tell those lies on your résumé, kiss all those behinds, and trample over all those people on your way to the top just so *someone else* can take over your job? I don't think so.

You say, "But everybody has to retire sometime. Or if not retire, at least die."

Not me, my friends. And if you're smart, not you.

You've got the power. You've got to hold on to it till your dying day. And when you do die—and personally, I'm not at all convinced that's going to happen to me—you should leave your organization in such disarray that no one will be able to take your place. Now that's a legacy. That will get you remembered for all time, when your company goes belly-up soon after you do. And immortality is only your just due.

But your immortality is for another book. Let's get back to the matter at hand: keeping power out of the hands of those who *think* they have a shot at eventually succeeding you.

It's easier than you think.

The Key to Power-Sucking

The most important thing to remember in dealing with your senior and junior managers is to *keep them off balance*. Your managers will pose much less of a threat to you when they are off balance (and, of course, will be naturally much easier to knock down, when need be).

Strong, secure managers is the last thing you want. Bewildered, confused managers is the first.

What you're looking to do is to keep your managers in a *permanent state of unease*. Uneasy managers will be kept far too busy trying to cover themselves and maintain their positions, and thus expend less energy trying to dethrone you. At the same time they're producing for you—supervising the rabble and other revolting tasks you don't like to dirty your hands with—they'll be looking nervously over their shoulders. It's truly the ideal situation for you.

But it's a high-wire act. To keep these people productive, you want them to think they're moving forward in the company. But you don't want them to be *sure*. So the only thing left for them to do is to keep working, holding on to the vague thought that they're advancing within the organization.

It's crucial that they never discover that the best they can do within your organization is to move *sideways*.

STRATEGIES FOR POWER-SUCKING

Here are a few methods I use to keep my managers busy, nervous, and in their proper hierarchical positions—below me, and buzzing around each other aimlessly.

Musical Managers

Musical Managers is one of the most effective ways I know to keep my top people rattled. With Musical Managers, these poor saps don't know whether they're coming or going.

What I do is shuffle managers from department to department, leaving them in one place just long enough to get a feel for the job. Then I transfer them to another department, let them get a feel for *that* job, then ship 'em off someplace else.

So, for example, I put Manager X in charge of Promotions. After six months, I then rocket X off to Accounting, replacing Manager B, who had finally gotten the hang of Accounting. I send B off to Production, where B is absolutely clueless. And so on and so forth. The key is to keep shuffling that deck.

I tell my managers this is to keep them "fresh" and "stimulated" and other BS straight from the *Caring Manager's Manual.*

What it's really for is to keep them totally confused and—you got it—*off balance.* There's nothing so disconcerting as to get used to something new, get good at it, and then have someone pull the rug right out from under you. It's a real confidence shatterer! And people with shattered confidence don't fool with the Big Cheese. That, my friends, I guarantee.

Added benefits: Different tasks and challenges actually do "stimulate" many of these people, who often come up with good administrative ideas for their new departments. So when I boot these people out, I steal their ideas and implement them in the departments myself. Thus I have a constant flow of new ideas for *all* my departments.

And when I claim authorship of these exciting innovations, nobody argues with me. Because anybody who argues knows that I'll be extremely happy to knock him or her right off that fast track to the top of our organization.

And here's the wonderful Catch-22 to all this: There *is* no fast track to the top of our organization. No matter what, my managers are always going to be stuck on a treadmill to nowhere. They're just rolling their wheels, like hamsters in a cage. I throw them little pieces of lettuce now and then to keep their legs moving, but they're never, ever going to even *smell* the power I've got.

Ah, Musical Managers. You do so many nice things for me.

Promises, Promises

In an old "Little Rascals" short, the gang drives a wagon that is pulled by a mule. They keep the mule moving by dangling a carrot on a string in front of its face, just out of reach of its mouth. Naturally, the mule never gets to the carrot but keeps going after it. And that wagon keeps rolling.

Pardon the grammar, but—*your managers are that mule.* And your promises are that carrot.

I'm not talking about your normal, everyday threats that *contain* promises, such as, "You shape up, or *I promise you* in your next job you'll be asking drink sizes." Or, "You get it done, or *I promise you* the next thing you'll be supervising is a production line of rubber vomit." You can always feel free to fulfill those kinds of promises. (As a matter of fact, it's a pleasure!)

And I'm certainly not talking about *specific* promises—e.g., "In January I'm making you head of production for the entire operation." You would have to be insane to make specific promises to any of the managers in your organization. These promises will *always* come back to haunt you. Many of these people got to where they are by being just as conniving and sneaky as you, and are more than willing to tape your conversations, bring forth surprise witnesses, and generally catch you in any falsehood you care to deliver. This can lead to some very embarrassing scenes and occasionally even annoying court battles.

> GOLDEN RULE: Never be specific about *any*
> job or position, in *any* time frame, to *any*one. These
> people are just dying to see you slip up so they can blow
> you out of the water. Don't hand 'em the buckshot!

No, what I'm talking about are those vague suggestions and remarks that will lead your top people to think you've got their welfare in mind. These are empty promises, *empty* because the shell of what you say appears to consist of a *promise* implied. But crack that shell and what have you got? That's right. Zippo. Nothing in there but hot air!

What I have is a master list of empty promises and bogus affirmations that I recycle for my top people day after day, week after week, month after month. I mix them up a little: I don't want Jones to hear the same baloney Smith heard a week before. Though, frankly, it doesn't really matter. It's just more fun and challenging to mix them up.

Feel free to use any of these to keep *your* managers jumping. Under each promise in parentheses is what I'm usually thinking as I deliver it—while trying to keep a straight face. Not always easy, believe me.

My Master List of Empty Promises and Bogus Affirmations
I've got plans for you.
   (Yeah, the plan is: There is no plan for you.)
You're on your way up.
   (Notice that I say this only while we're in an elevator.)
Patience is a virtue.
   (At least it is for you, you schmuck.)
Keep the faith.
   (Sure, why the hell not? Nothing wrong with keeping
   the faith.)

I see a promotion on the horizon.
   (Not *your* horizon, nitwit.)
They also serve, those who stand and wait.
   (Hahahahahaha…hohohohoho…Stop it…stop it,
   you're killin' me.)
You're going places.
   (Hey, everybody goes places. Maybe you're going to the
   grocery store later. Who knows?)
Don't worry, everything's going to be fine.
   (I'm talking about for me.)
My appreciation will take a more tangible form.
   (I'll have my secretary get you a card.)
Sit tight—you'll be rewarded for all you've done.
   (Although not by me.)
You'll be taken care of.
   (Although not the way you think.)
I've got my eye on you.
   (You'd best believe it.)

Divide and Conquer

Keeping your top people running around in circles while feeding them empty promises may be satisfying and amusing work, but sooner or later some of your veteran managers might begin questioning it. It's sad, but that's human nature. These people, instead of being filled with gratitude at the opportunity to work with you, might actually start to *resent* the fact that they've been spinning their wheels for so long in your organization.

This in itself is harmless. Frustrated individuals are no threat to you. But a frustrated *group*? Watch out, because it's true: United they stand.

So it's up to you to divide them.

What you have to do is *pit these people against one another.*

The good news is that this is almost laughably easy.

All it takes is a few well-placed divisive remarks. What these remarks need to contain are secondhand versions of complaints, slurs, or (on a good day) sleazy gossip that other managers have dished out about the particular person you're speaking to.

Say you're talking to Manager C. You mention oh-so-casually something rotten that Managers B and A said about C. You see C bristle. Bingo. That's all there is to it. You can be specific or general about who said what as you slip these bombs into the conversation. It doesn't matter. Either way, it will make your managers squirm.

Think of these remarks as tiny seeds you're planting in these people's minds, seeds that will eventually flower into full-grown doubts, suspicions, and animosities. They have to be made off-hand, sometimes even in passing. You're the boss and are above such petty and malicious office gossip. But a discreet word from you here and there can keep it flowing—and keep your managers at each other's throats. Most certainly, away from yours.

You ask, "What if my managers don't say anything negative or damaging about each other in my presence?"

Well, then, it's time to put on the old thinking cap and make some stuff up! You can choose from any category: (a) Ineptitude or Incompetence on the Job; (b) Drug Abuse; (c) Brownnosing; (d) Sexual Perversion—you get the idea. Use your imagination!

Don't forget: You've got unassailable credibility. It won't often occur to these people that the slander you're repeating is sheer invention on your part. They're going to be far too busy dealing with their rampant paranoia—or they'll be out for blood.

Chew on these never-fail divisive remarks. I think you'll find them very tasty.

Divisive Remarks: The Classics

"They're wrong, Warren. You *do* know your ass from second base."

"Morton suggested your mood swings are due to medication. Well, we can't let your department fall apart just because you need to be medicated."

"Remember, DeVita, just because you cooperate with me does *not* make you an ass kisser, brownnoser, butt boy, or whatever else it is they happen to be calling you this week."

"And Browning and Pettite say you're clueless. I don't think so."

"You know, Jackson, just because you don't grasp a concept the instant you hear it doesn't necessarily make you an imbecile. Why do I listen to that Reeves anyway!"

"Is it true you're setting your department back five years, or is *everybody* wrong?"

"Of course others are going to say your problems are cocaine-driven, but I'm not buying that."

"So from all accounts you like your little drinky-winkys."

"Since time began people like you who happen to enjoy the beautiful gift of sex have been called sluts. Personally, I think Hawkins is jealous."

"Go ahead, speak freely, Robertson. It isn't *me* who thinks you're a stinking stool pigeon."

MEETINGS: POWER-SUCKING IN A GROUP ATMOSPHERE

We all know meetings are basically worthless. Nothing ever gets done in meetings. They're a joke.

However, meetings *can* be useful for further cementing the hierarchy (you up; everyone else down) in your organization, and for the superb opportunities they afford you to discomfit your managers further. After all, a meeting is one of the few times when you can have your top people together in one room, giving you a clear shot to make the whole gaggle of them sweat in unison.

Today's Agenda
As the leader of your company, it's up to you to set the agenda in your company's meetings.

My agenda is quite simple: *This is my company and my meeting. Don't do or say anything here that will make me hurt you.* Before all my meetings, I print out this agenda and circulate it among all the members of the group.

Many management books tell you that meetings are valuable so you can hear different points of view—ones that even might be contrary to your own.

I say that if my managers disagree with me, they'll pay the penalty. Maybe not now, but soon, and for the rest of their lives.

I will on occasion immediately "share my feelings" when my managers do disagree with or displease me. In some meetings, for example, when I hear something I don't like from one of my managers, I ring an Idiot Bell that I bring along with me. A few of these sessions, as you might imagine, have sounded like a Sunday morning in a hick Iowa town.

But the Idiot Bell is really just a cornball prop. I use it only when I'm in a foul mood. I'm not in a foul mood often. I actually have quite a rosy view of things—which isn't hard when you're holding all the cards.

No, to shake up my top people in meetings I generally use more subtle techniques.

Staring
While a manager is delivering a departmental report in a meeting,

I stare intently at someone, nearly burning a hole in my subject. "You're staring at the manager giving the report?" you ask.

No. I'll be staring at *another* manager—I pick any old one—who would normally be sitting and daydreaming, half listening to his or her colleague—that is, until he or she gets a load of the boss glaring at them. Then they perspire, fidget, and sometimes emit little moans. These people have just made an unscheduled stop in Hot Seat, Arkansas, and believe me, they're *never* ready for it.

Not only that, the manager who is attempting to speak is so rattled by the boss inexplicably staring fixedly at another member of the group that the report invariably peters out into nothing. Which is fine. I never listen to those things anyway. But this still gives me the opportunity to say at the end of the presentation: "Well, Curtis. Not terribly prepared today, were we?"

Distracting Physical Movements
While a meeting is in session, I make others tense and uncomfortable with my body language. Waving my hand in front of my face as if brushing away a fly, raising myself up on my haunches and looking wildly around, carefully examining my nails or playing elaborate games with my cuff links, and gazing dully off into space like a psychotic in a courtroom are all extremely effective ways to send the message, *I am bored.* This gives my people a vague notion that they're doing something wrong. Which they probably are.

Occasionally in the middle of a presentation or proposal, I like to stand up, straighten my tie, run my hand over my scalp, and then walk out of the room, never to return. When my managers come up to me later and ask if it was something they said, I merely reply, "You tell me. Do *you* think it was something you said?"

As I rarely have a clue as to what they said—I'm often working the stock market on my laptop during these things—their by now fully developed paranoia will naturally take over.

Added benefits: Paranoia is a tremendous spur for your managers to come up with better ideas. *Paranoia* is *production.* Never forget: You can make these better ideas your own.

Non Sequiturs

I've also found the use of non sequiturs, carefully placed within a discussion, effectively sabotages any of my managers' notions that they are "getting somewhere" ("somewhere" meaning closer to the top). Just as they get on a roll, I knock them right off their pins. For instance:

MANAGER: So, all in all, if we fully develop our on-line revenue sources, I believe it's realistic to expect that we can not only meet our budget for next year, but even come out a little ahead of the game. Looking at the preliminary numbers, we can all be encouraged that—

ME: If the city salts the sidewalks this winter like they did last winter, I'll have to start treating my shoes in October. But then again, I can always wear rubbers.

MANAGER: Ah...yes, sir. Um...we can all be encouraged that our projections—

ME: Paprika on deviled eggs? Hasn't that been done to death?

MANAGER: Yes, sir.

ME: Rotation is the key to long tire life. There's no arguing that point.

MANAGER (*wearily*): No, sir.

GOLDEN RULE: Keeping your top management guessing, bewildered, and confused *while still producing* is the absolute essential in maintaining a death grip on your power.

MOTIVATION—IF YOU MUST

Motivating people is the simplest thing in the world. Here's the formula every leader needs to remember:

EMPLOYEE DOES JOB AS DICTATED BY YOU = EMPLOYEE KEEPS JOB

EMPLOYEE DOESN'T DO JOB AS DICTATED BY YOU= EMPLOYEE LOSES JOB

Isn't this formula beautiful? So simple, so true, like a Norman Rockwell painting of a boss, cigar clenched between his teeth, informing some poor sap that he's been fired and is being replaced by a chimpanzee. Lovelier than a portrait of a doe lapping water from a mountain stream—right in a hunter's sights and about to be blasted to kingdom come.

It's a formula that's been lost in American business lately. And I'm here to tell you "that sucks," as today's punks say.

The sad fact is that many business leaders have been brainwashed into believing outlandish theories put forth by certain management gurus. The espousal of praise, communication, teamwork, inclusion, and other nauseating concepts as motivational factors has overwhelmed good old-fashioned horse sense in running a business.

My friends, the nausea stops here.

FEAR: YOUR VERY BEST BUDDY

Many books tell managers that fear is never a proper motivator when it comes to getting employees to produce. They say that the use of fear spurs low morale and bitter resentment of management among workers. I beg to differ.

Fear is the surefire key to motivating people. There's really nothing like it to make them jump through hoops. As for low morale and resentment . . . *that's really not your problem.* Don't give it a second thought.

However, if you insist on considering the effect your policy of fear has on drones, look at the bright side: If an employee is unhappy and openly resentful of you while in your employ, then you have every right to fire said employee.

That made you feel better, didn't it? I knew it would.

• *An example of using fear to goose slackers:* Just the other day, I encountered an employee whom I had been informed was not pulling her weight in her department. I called her into my office. Sliding my office door shut with its satisfying clang—a door I had imported from a cellblock at the Lucasville, Ohio, penitentiary—I told her to sit down.

"Jane," I said, "I've noticed that your sales are way down this past quarter. You've been a fairly productive worker in the past. Do you have any explanation for this slump you're in?"

Jane, who told me that her name wasn't Jane but Eileen— not a smart idea on her part, by the way, to contradict me— proceeded to go into a long song and dance about her "health" and "state of mind" and that there were several "issues" she had to "resolve" in her "personal life."

"Jane," I said, "that's all very fascinating. But here's an issue I have to resolve in *my* personal life.

"What do I do with a slacker who's not contributing to the company? I can't pay her any more. I can't let her mooch around the office, bothering my other workers. Nor can I in

good conscience write her a letter of recommendation after she's gone. How can I let her victimize some other company—a company that most likely employs people *I play golf with*—and still look myself in the eye? How can I not call everyone I know, and not tell them that she's a credit risk? If this ruins her and her family's lives, you have to remember that there's a bigger issue at stake here: *the issue of my own integrity.* I'm torn, Jane."

Do you see how I twisted Jane's problems to (a) totally invalidate their importance; and (b) make them my own, spinning them around to contrive some phony-baloney but highly effective "integrity" issue I had to deal with? Of course this was pure crapola—I would have ratted Jane out for the sheer pleasure of it—but she didn't know that.

After our talk, Jane's health and state of mind improved dramatically and her problems were miraculously resolved. I've used this strategy with dozens of employees like Jane—and have helped them like I helped her. Threatening the little people to get their asses in gear is one of the most rewarding things you can do as a manager.

Most important, I helped *me.* Following our little chat, Jane's sales skyrocketed, and I never heard another word from her about her "personal issues." Just as it should be.

Slaves will pick more succulent figs if they are threatened with disembowelment if they don't. They'll pick those succulent figs big time.
    —Common saying among landowners of ancient Rome

THE PERILS OF PRAISE
The trouble with praising functionaries is that if you praise them once, they'll expect it again…and again…and again. You simply can't have that. Because then they get "ideas."

Say an employee does a creditable job on an assigned project, a presentation to a prospective client, for example. When he or she hands the project over to you for your approval, and you find it satisfactory (something that won't happen often), the worst thing you can say is, "Excellent job."

When you say "excellent job" to an underling, then this individual feels that he or she is "excellent." Of course, this is utter nonsense. A cog in the wheel, maybe. A link in the chain, perhaps. A drone in the hive, surely. But "excellent"?

No way. *You* are excellent. Your employees are merely present to do their jobs, go to their little homes, watch their little TV shows, and then die. That's it. You tell them that they did an "excellent job" and they'll begin to question this very basic precept of American working life.

That's not good management. The next thing you know, they'll want *your* job. Is this what they call "motivation"?

All you need to do when someone hands you their assigned work is say, "Just give me that thing." On that extremely rare occasion when you're in a giddy mood or you want to supply a slight boost, you may say, "All right. Now get back to work."

GOLDEN RULE: Encouraging employees is the first step on the road to communism.

THE JOY OF CONSTRUCTIVE CRITICISM

One of the things I do on a daily basis in my role as leader is make the rounds of the office, stopping at each desk and inscribing a large red *X* on any document or piece of paper my underlings happen to be working on. At computer terminals, I simply highlight the material and hit the "delete" key.

I don't need to know what it is I'm marking or deleting. What my employees need to know is that I consider their work *unacceptable*.

It makes no difference what the work is. It makes no difference if I've read it. Here is precisely what the Big Red X and the Big Bad Delete mean:

I am in charge. You are a peon. Your work is no good. Do it again.

This is called constructive criticism.

Constructive criticism is essential in motivating employees to do their very best work. There's nothing more devastating than having hours and hours of your work destroyed by a management Magic Marker scrawling an *X* or an Executive Finger pressing a button on a computer keyboard. The threat of this keeps your employees on their toes, right where they belong. And an *alert* employee is a *fully functioning* employee.

You've taught me well, Teresa —Jo—

Constructive Criticism: Pleasures and Payoffs

When I was a senior manager, a young up-and-comer—we'll call him Jim—brought me a brilliant proposal to streamline our interoffice communications system. I read it, growing more impressed with each idea.

"Well, Jim," I said. "This is interesting. But I do have some criticism of your ideas."

I then called in my secretary, and gave it to her to copy. *Yet I didn't tell Jim I was doing this.* I hid his proposal among some other papers that I had handed to my secretary. Jim and I made small talk about sports and movies we had seen until my secretary returned.

I took Jim's original proposal, marked a big red *X* on it with my executive Magic Marker, and coldly ordered him out of my office. Jim slithered out, one surprised smarty-pants.

I then implemented all of Jim's ideas, improved our communications system tenfold, and got all the credit. When Jim squawked and tried to sandbag me, I rigged his urine test to make up a potent crack-cocaine cocktail. I moved *up,* and Jim moved *out.*

Do you see how effective well-placed criticism can be? This same strategy works just fine for me as CEO. The difference is that now nobody complains.

"TEAMS" AND THE MYTH OF "INCLUSION"

Many management gurus insist that employees should be "included" as part of a "team." This, they tell us, will make them happier and, thus, more productive.

Well, I say this: If they want to join a team, tell them to try out for the Dallas Cowboys. You're in business here. This isn't some schoolroom where we all go out together on field trips to the park and buy each other cartons of yogurt and watch some mime make an ass of himself. It's every man, woman, and child for himself, and there isn't enough room on the lifeboats for everybody. You think the survivors of the *Titanic* formed "teams"? I don't. I think they hustled. I think they moved. I think they *got the hell out of there.*

But some people seem to believe that we should all get together and form "teams" and "focus groups." Then we should "include," "diversify," "talk," "mentor," "make group decisions," and other notions too sickening to contemplate.

The next thing you know, that punk fresh out of college who's been with the organization eight months begins to think he's on your level and wants you to "open" your books and give everyone the chance to take a gander at them. Because this is what we're ultimately talking about.

As Clint Eastwood said in *In the Line of Fire, "That's not gonna happen."*

Clint was talking about the attempted assassination of the

president of the United States, but I'm talking about something far worse: the inmates taking over the asylum, the chimps taking over the monkey house.

And that, my friends, has never been a terribly sound management strategy.

The minute any of your managers even breathes a word about "teams," you have to transform, like magic, this manager into an ex-manager and, ultimately, ex-employee. Because if you don't, he'll form a team, all right—he'll team up with other managers to make sure your ass is out on the street and his is sitting behind your desk, smoking your Cubans and drinking your Cutty.

Is that plain enough for you?

Don't waste your time on teams.

"Include" This

If people want to feel "included"—to be more a part of the company and its future—you have to make them believe. You have to make them believe that if they don't do what you say, they have no future with the company.

This is a relatively simple thing to accomplish within an organization. A few well-placed words to an individual—or to a group—can make a world of difference in making underlings feel they are integral components of your business.

To the individual: Jones, do as I say or you're fired.

To the group: Hey, everybody, do as I say or you're fired.

See? In this way functionaries feel *included.* They're included in a process: the process of working under you, performing tasks you wish them to perform at your pleasure, and generally placing their tiny lives in the palm of your hand.

It's difficult to get any more included than that.

SENDING THE MESSAGE

Sometimes, however, the classic "Do it or you're gone" line isn't quite enough. There will be times you will be required to make a speech that inspires and instills a message to your employees. Why this is necessary—these people are being *paid,* after all—is open for debate. But I've found that on occasion taking the podium and delivering edicts to the peasants can be quite stimulating.

When it's time to speak inspirationally to a group, remember who you're talking to. These people are nothing like you. In other words, this is one not-very-bright group.

Therefore, things need to be stated in the simplest possible terms. While your speeches don't need to quite be on the level of "See Dick run; run, Dick, run," they shouldn't be too much more complex.

The following is an excerpt from a speech I made to my company's sales force just a few months ago.

"This past quarter, your sales have dropped nearly one-half of one percent. Acceptable? No. Sales go up or people go bye-bye? Yes. Now get back to work."

Note: Some management books insist that you use the pronoun *we* when speaking to employees. (There's that notion of "inclusion" again.) The only time you need to use the word *we* is when you're discussing you, your superiors (if any), and your community's police department: e.g., "We have decided you will be required to work fourteen-hour days Monday through Friday" and "We have no hesitation in placing any of you under arrest and prosecuting you to the fullest extent of the law if there are any disturbances resulting from this matter."

Nonverbal Messages in Speeches and Encounters with Underlings

I've been told that successful executives "open" their faces while speaking to employees, thus imparting "optimism" and "enthusiasm." They make direct eye contact, stand up straight, grin, and generally burble over like Kathie Lee Gifford pumping the latest Hollywood half-wit.

Fine. Do that. Except consider one thing. That kind of behavior sends one message, and one message only: that you *enjoy* relating to peons.

These people have to realize they are taking up your valuable time, and that an audience with you is something they have to work for and arrange well in advance. Like the Wizard of Oz, you have to cultivate inaccessibility. Do you really want people to *believe* that your "door is always open"?

You send nonverbal messages like that and you'll be getting telephone calls at *home,* my friend. What next? Are you going to give them your PIN number? Unlimited use of your American Express card? The keys to your Lexus? The name of your connection for those wonderful, inexpensive Haitian servants you so enjoy ordering about your house?

I have one nonverbal message, and it's fitted snugly in a fine leather holster inside my jacket. When I unbutton my jacket, the little people see it. And that's one nonverbal message they truly do understand.

Memos That Motivate

You might get the idea that I'm suggesting that you hole up in your office and never make an appearance in front of the commoners.

On the contrary. It's absolutely essential that these people know you're "around." But your physical presence is not necessarily required for this to be accomplished.

One method I use with employees to let them know that I am indeed around is the calculated and strategic use of memos.

The memos I send to underlings are short and sweet. They

tell a story. They send a message. But they never have anything to do with anything specific. You don't want them to get their grubby mitts on anything specific because that's an invitation for them to mount a "defense" of their actions. And you can't have that. (For when underlings do commit specific violations, see the next chapter, "Punishment.") So all of my memos are form memos, prewritten but personalized to the grunt I'm sending it to.

Here's an example of a typical memo I just shot off a few moments ago:

MEMO
TO: Elizabeth Rogers
FROM: Your Employer
Mr. or Ms. Rogers:
I'm watching you.
Y.E. (signed)

Isn't that a beauty? As far as I know, Ms. Rogers does her job adequately, toes the line, slinks home every evening at 5 P.M., and draws her pittance every two weeks. To tell the truth, I wouldn't know Ms. Rogers if I fell over her.

But I want Ms. Rogers to know something. *I'm watching her.* That's it. I'm watching her, and others like her. All the time.

Here are a few of the other, standardized messages I send to various functionaries on a regular basis:

- No one is indispensable.
- Get to work.
- It's humiliating to be replaced by a weighted brick or a trained chicken.
- The walls have ears.
- Look out.
- Suffering brings redemption.

- How long have you been in my employ?
- I understand you have a family.
- The good die young.
- The night has a thousand eyes.
- How much do you earn per week?
- Downsizing begins in the most unexpected places.

I also have a font on my word processor that approximates the look of words written in blood when I want to get that *extra special* point across. Extremely effective.

REWARDS

Reward a fool; reward a folly. Or, reward a folly; reward a fool. Listen, just don't reward anybody.
—Sir Edmund Dithering, 1578

Unfortunately, when you're not the top dog of your company, you may find yourself receiving instructions from misguided souls up above that employees who do a good job should be "rewarded" in some manner beyond a paycheck. And that this, too, provides motivation.

I know, I know, but it happens. Not everyone can be CEO right off the bat, and you're bound to have to put up with a little nonsense on the way up. I remember having to grit my teeth and follow the directions of more than a few "healers" and "nurturers" who believed in the rewards system.

So I did it. I rewarded. It hurt. But I did it.

And when I eventually became senior to the wimps, I rewarded them, too. Rewarded them right out the door, and most likely into one of those crybaby support groups they're so fond of forming with other unemployed managers. Where they can blubber and whine and give each other big wet hugs. That's fine; they're happy there.

But what about you, who's being ordered to dole out rewards like some corporate Santa Claus?

Relatively Pain-Free Rewarding

When you're told to give an employee a reward for a job well done, there are several routes you can take. I've found the following to be far more palatable than the alternative that some espouse—e.g., sizable cash bonuses—which you'd have to be crazy to give.

• *Memos.* A congratulatory memo will often serve as sufficient reward.

I remember one occasion when an employee named Mary Hargrove turned the sales of our company around single-handedly with one of the most ingenious publicity campaigns I've ever seen. She labored for weeks on this project in her off hours, presented it to us, and we flew with it, making a huge splash in the papers and on TV and radio. Sales skyrocketed and the company immediately achieved a higher profile and became more profitable than ever.

Because Mary Hargrove did exactly what a functionary is supposed to do—make her boss look good—I rewarded her with this memo:

> TO: Mary Hargrove
> FROM: Your Superior
> Mr. or Ms. Hargrove:
> You did an adequate job on the publicity business. Now get back to work.
> Y.S. (signed)

Because I was particularly pleased with Ms. Hargrove's work, I took the unprecedented step of circling the "Ms." in the salutation, making her feel even more like a "person."

Yes, Ms. Hargrove knew I was one happy camper.

• *Small gifts.* On extraordinary occasions, I have even felt moved to present a particularly productive drone with a small gift.

I recall one fellow named Howard Kleinman performing a miraculous job researching and advising us in installing a computer system, saving the company hundreds of thousands of dollars in the process.

So I went to a nearby discount drugstore and bought Kleinman a plastic pocket comb. I didn't break the bank—it cost under a dollar—but the comb was unbreakable as well as handsome. So happy was I with Kleinman I even included a memo along with the comb, with this message:

"You did an adequate job on the computer business. You may take a moment off to enjoy your comb. Then get back to work."

• *The occasional—and I mean occasional—cash reward.* When an employee does a stellar job on an assignment, I have in rare instances placed a shiny new quarter on his or her desk. The problem with this type of reward is that people will expect it again and again. First a quarter, then fifty cents—before you know it, you're handing out dollar bills like penny candy. But that's what "rewards" get you.

Let's move on to something more pleasant: how to punish these people adequately when they don't toe the line.

PUNISHMENT: THIS TIME, IT'S PERSONAL

Punish the person, not the act.
                    —Howard R. Feral, Feral Investments
Punishment makes the world go 'round.
                    —Mahatma Gandhi, at some point, I'm sure

Despite your most heartfelt and sincere efforts to keep your employees beaten down and producing, you obviously can't be everywhere at once, constantly checking up on them to make sure they're toeing the line.

Certainly company spies, moles, and the strategic placement of surveillance cameras help toward this end, but, believe me, these people know how to get around anything. Like children or not-yet-housebroken puppies, they will defiantly and willfully misbehave. And unfortunately, a sharp rap on their snout with your finger won't always do the trick.

So what *do* you do when you discover that your employees are violating company policy that you, through your bountiful wisdom and experience, have set down for them to mindlessly (if you'll excuse the redundancy) follow and obey?

What do you do when they take advantage of you and cruelly exploit your random acts of decency—which, after all, you're *under no obligation* to perform?

What do you do when their natural animal indolence takes over, rendering them about as productive to your organization as those far-too-expensive-and-comfortable chairs they fill with their slumping carcasses all day?

Not that this should occur too often. No, not *too* often.

News bulletin: Half of most of your employees' day is dedicated to breaking the rules of your office. The other half is dedicated to completely avoiding doing any meaningful work.

One moment you'll see them staring dully off into space, their minds occupied with that week's episode of *Melrose Place,* or they'll be calculating how to sneak that illicit Little Debbie cupcake they've squirreled away in their top drawer. And the next moment they'll be in the rest rooms, gossiping away with each other *on your time,* and probably flushing unauthorized items down the toilets.

This is precisely why they are who they are, and why you are who *you* are. Their function in the world is to violate company policy and, when not occupying themselves with that, to goof off. Your function in the world is to *punish* them when they do. And punish them you must.

I'll let you savor that thought a moment before we go on.

PERSONALIZED PUNISHMENT

Some management experts feel that predetermined disciplinary actions and reprimands should be set for every conceivable offense, so that you will be fair and even-handed.

But do you really want some *book* to tell you what to do when these people screw up, as they invariably will? Where's the creativity in that? Where's the fun?

As the finest prison wardens know, the best punishment is one that fits the crime. This is why you must enforce *personalized punishment.* It takes a little imagination to come up with personalized punishment, but it's worth the effort. What sublime pleasure to see that pitiful, forlorn expression on some sap's face—*Busted! Big time!*—as he experiences a punishment tailored specifically to him.

Come along with me through a catalog of offenses, and I'll show you how I've punished various miscreants—and in a personal way.

Note: In all these cases I was asked to intervene by my managers when they couldn't handle the transgressors. They had tried to "reason" with these people, to use "gentle persuasion"—on their way to "nurturing" them and "respecting their dignity."

When that flopped, they called me.

Tardy Tony

For the life of him, Tony just couldn't seem to make it to the office on time. While all the other drones managed to scrape their way in before or at 8:30 A.M., Tony never seemed to arrive until several minutes past 9. It seems Tony had a little trouble rousing himself in the morning to get up and go to work.

I thought I might give Tony a wake-up call.

I directed one of my larger associates to "ask" the superintendent of Tony's apartment building to give him copies of the keys to the building and to Tony's suite. Which my associate then handed to me.

Very early one morning, I slipped into Tony's building and then into his apartment. I tiptoed around until I found his bedroom, and I peered in. There was Tony, working far more diligently at nabbing forty winks than he ever did nabbing new business for the company.

ERIC BRODER

I sat on the end of Tony's bed and loudly cleared my throat.

Tony sleepily lifted his right eyelid, and suddenly the previously inert (and obviously nonproductive) shape under the blanket jumped.

"Whuh…whuh," said Tony, blinking rapidly.

I said to Tony, "I'm Mr. Getum Upp, here to nudge you out of bed and wipe the sleep from your eyes. Mr. Getum Upp likes to assist those who are chronically late in arriving at the workplace.

"Here's an interesting side note: Did you know Mr. Getum Upp has the power to terminate your employment and cut off your benefits?" I pulled out a large hunting knife and slowly moved my finger along its razor-sharp edge. "You wouldn't want me to cut off your benefits, would you?"

I got up and walked to the bedroom door. Then I turned.

"This dream is over, punk."

Watercooler Connie

Oh, Connie, Connie, Connie. Connie dearly loved to drink more than her allotted single Dixie cup–full of the expensive bottled water I supplied underlings out of the goodness of my heart. I don't know why employees need water, but in a weak moment I was convinced by a junior manager that they did. So I invested in a watercooler.

Who knew Connie would make such a water pig of herself?

I had been told by my cooler informants that on one day alone Connie guzzled down three full cups of water—*nearly fourteen ounces of liquid.*

I immediately removed the watercooler. I then made up a sign and posted it where the cooler used to stand:

DRINKING WATER WILL NOW BE AVAILABLE ONLY FROM THE TAP ON THE NORTH EXTERIOR OF THE BUILDING. YOU MAY PUT YOUR MOUTH TO THE SPOUT AND GET A DRINK ONLY WHEN AUTHORIZED IN WRITING BY A SUPERIOR. THIS SPOT WILL BE KNOWN AS CONNIE'S PLACE, IN HONOR OF CONNIE MORRISON OF SALES, WHOSE GLUTTONY IS RESPONSIBLE FOR THE REMOVAL OF THE WATERCOOLER FORMERLY IN THIS AREA. NOW STOP READING AND GET BACK TO WORK.

Connie may have been many things after the watercooler incident, but no one ever mistook her for Ms. Popularity.

Copyin' Craig

My goodness, Craig surely did like making copies! Unnecessary copies. Extraneous copies. Expensive copies. Unauthorized and *personal* copies.

Craig just wouldn't *stop* making so many copies, even when directed to do so by his superiors. He'd just wave them off, saying, "Oh, the company can afford it. I got to copy this stuff for my rotisserie baseball league."

You might say Craig had designated himself the ruler of the copy machine. So I decided to reward Craig. I set up a chair right next to the copier, and put a sign over it:

KING CRAIG OF THE COPY MACHINE

ONLY THE KING PERMITTED TO MAKE COPIES ON THIS MACHINE

You'll find Craig sitting there today, wearing his little cardboard crown, making copies for everyone, on demand. And let me tell you: It's one full-time job!

I'm not sure Craig is happy being King of the Copy Machine, but here's something I've known that Craig knows now, too.

Lonely is the head that wears the Copy Crown.

Sickly Sarah

Poor Sarah. Sarah just couldn't stay healthy enough to come to work and do her job. Sarah took more sick days than everyone else in the office combined. Sarah made Camille look like a piker.

Problem was, Sarah was often spotted in various malls around town power-shopping when she was supposedly languishing on her sickbed. She went about her business with amazing energy and enthusiasm for someone so enfeebled with disease.

So one day I had various associates station themselves at the boutiques Sarah was fond of patronizing while she courageously battled her serious illnesses. And when my associate spotted her at one, I was called. There was no problem keeping her there, because you couldn't blast Sarah out of her favorite shop with a grenade.

I drove over to the shop, went to the checkout counter, slipped the cashier a twenty, got behind the counter, and kept my back turned until Sarah was ready to make her purchase. When she handed me her purchase—a charming little brown leather clutch—I said, "That will be all for you today."

Sarah, not looking up and thinking she had been asked a question, replied, "Yes, that's all." Suddenly something awful dawned on her, and she did look up. I smiled pleasantly at her.

"That will be all for you today."

After her day of shopping, Sarah's health took a miraculous turn for the better, and we were all so pleased at the office with her improved attendance.

Howard the Hippie

Howard knew the dress code. It was stated explicitly. Dark suit. Light blue or white shirt. Solid-color or—on holidays only—conservative-pattern necktie. Black shoes. *At all times.*

But one day Howard came into the office wearing a blue blazer. Khaki slacks. White button-down shirt with blue stripes, and red madras tie. And brown loafers...with tassels.

Perhaps Howard thought he was going to Woodstock, or to some mosh pit. Or perhaps Howard was thinking of joining "Generation X" or becoming a "slacker" (no stretch for him there).

No one could guess what Howard was thinking. The only thing that was clear was that Howard was not dressed for work. Howard was dressed for the circus. Which gave me an idea.

We told Howard that we were going to "loosen up" at the office and have a Big Top Day, where all the employees would come in dressed as their favorite circus performers. I sweetened the pot by saying that the best costumes would win considerable cash prizes, there would be plenty of booze available, and we'd all generally "kick out the jams." Howard's tiny rat eyes lit up at the prospect.

So on the appointed day Howard showed up dressed like a clown, complete with flaming orange wig and red nose, garish mouth and eye makeup, a huge yellow collar over a bright blue one-piece outfit, and of course the famous floppy shoes.

Needless to say, no one else was similarly dressed. Howard looked around in confusion. The expression on his face at that moment gave him an uncanny resemblance to that perpetually sad clown Emmett Kelly.

I went up to Howard and said, "What the hell do you think you're doing?" Howard began babbling about "Big Top Day" and "costumes" and "beer" and "prizes," to which I coldly responded, "Do you really think I'd permit that here?"

However, I should admit that this was one ruse that somewhat backfired. Howard was apparently so taken by his Big Top get-up he scrapped his job at the company and enrolled at a clown university.

I suppose our loss was Barnum and Bailey's gain.

Aah, not really.

Defecatin' Dan

I can't say Dan ever did much actual work for our organization, but he was unsurpassed at one function: defecating on company time.

Twice in the morning, three times in the afternoon. You might say it was a hobby with Dan. I was more familiar with Dan's feet from the perspective of seeing them under a bathroom stall than attached to Dan upright and working.

Possibly Dan had a medical condition, you say. Perhaps Dan couldn't help it.

No, Dan just liked sitting on the can. It was peaceful in there. He wasn't required to work. The toilet is not a demanding taskmaster. It just sits there. Like Dan.

I was told I couldn't brick up the rest rooms—some health-code nonsense. And, to be fair, some of my other employees did have to urinate and defecate occasionally, though I still don't quite understand why it had to be done on my time. You defecate once in the morning at home, you lay off the liquids during the day, you're fine. What was I running here? A nursing home?

However, it's not realistic to expect that kind of discipline and self-control from these people. I'd rather have them commit their filthy business in a rest room than in the corner of the office. I wasn't about to let them turn my office space into Calcutta.

As for Dan, the solution was simple. I put a tape recorder in his favorite stall, hiding it behind the toilet. It caught all his moaning, whistling, and humming—not to mention his disgusting eruptions. When Dan came back to his desk after his pause that refreshed, the tape was playing for the whole office, at full volume.

How did the luckless Dan know it was him being recorded? Because Dan, and only Dan, whistled "Tara's Theme" from *Gone With the Wind* while perched on the throne.

As God is my witness, Dan never defecated in my organization again.

Lazy Louise

Louise of Sales just didn't seem to have the enthusiasm for her job that was necessary for her to fulfill its obligations. She seemed listless and unmotivated. She didn't seem to be enjoying the *challenges* of her work. Consequently, her production was way down to an unacceptable level.

Louise was lazier than hell. She didn't do jack.

In the old days, you simply booted out the Louises of the world and told them never to darken your door again. However, in these litigious times you have to be more creative.

So I brought in an old friend, Franklin D. Barker, Jr. Franklin D. Barker, Jr., is a midget and an actor who specializes in masquerading as a small child. He's uncanny. You can't tell the difference between him and an actual five-year-old.

I told Louise that Franklin—or "Toby"—was the son of a business associate, and that I promised my associate I'd let Toby try his hand at sales, as an experiment.

Louise said, "You're going to let a *child* make sales calls?"

"Yes," I replied. "And you're going to train him." Toby, his small hand in mine, squirmed, babbled, and generally did the toddler shtick.

Louise didn't like this one bit, but she did as she was told.

I watched as Louise instructed Toby on the finer points of composing sales letters, making cold calls, and pitching prospective clients. Toby nodded vigorously at everything she said.

After an hour of Louise's "training," he cried, "Lemme try it!" He jumped up and down. "Lemme *try* it!"

Louise gave Toby the phone number of a potential advertiser she'd been calling for two years with absolutely no luck and who had actually threatened to sue her for harassment. I felt this was rather petty of Louise. I don't think she cared for Toby at all.

She liked him even less when he very quickly got a six-month contract out of the formerly reluctant advertiser. Toby kissed ass, bullshitted, flattered, sucked up, made ridiculous promises, and generally swept this advertiser off his feet as if he'd done it all his life.

Which he had. Franklin D. Barker, Jr., is also a noted motivational speaker and author of the phenomenal *New York Times* best-seller *Close that Deal in Forty Seconds or Less: Sales When You're in a Hurry.*

Toby hung up the phone and said to Louise, "I got it! Can you write it up? I dunno how to write yet. I gotta go potty."

I kept Toby on for another week. He closed about seventy sales during that period, as Louise watched in amazement. Then I told Louise that Toby was starting kindergarten shortly and would no longer be with us.

As it turned out, neither was Louise. She told me that her ability to train a tot to sell was a sure sign that she should get into the business of motivational speaking and leading sales seminars. She was obviously herself a sales genius.

"So you can take this job and shove it up your ass," Louise

told me. "In six months I'll be able to buy and sell you, creep."
My goodness! I just didn't have the heart to tell her.

I watched Louise follow her dream, which, after many
twists and turns, eventually—and inevitably—led to her current
position as a server at a popular family restaurant that specializes
in ice cream desserts and burgers that you can fashion yourself
with a wide range of toppings.

Really delicious.

GOLDEN RULE: Employees remember you
far better for how you *punish* them than for how you
reward them. Make sure to punish them good.

EMPLOYEES AS "PEOPLE"

*One day I noticed what had once been a relatively functional
employee moping around the office. And I had heard through the
grapevine that for weeks he had not been producing anywhere near
the level he had before.*

"Dave," I asked him, "what seems to be your problem?"

*"Well," Dave replied in a trembling voice, "my wife left me
and took my two children with her. She just took off and left. There
was a note saying 'It's over,' and that was all.*

*"My wife and those kids were the lights of my life. I don't know
how I'll go on without them." I saw Dave's eyes well up at the
thought of his absent wife and children, and then he began to weep
openly.*

*"Dave," I said, "you better get your narrow little ass in gear
and back to work or I'll really give you something to cry about."*

—My dear friend Ray Hunt,
president and CEO, Goering Industries

The anecdote that opens this chapter is certainly amusing
on its surface, but I relate it to make a serious point.

Like it or not, most of the functionaries working under you have "human" characteristics—and some have them in spades!

Many are hotbeds of insecurities, anxieties, and fears. You, as boss, naturally contribute to some of these feelings, as well as to a variety of their physical ailments (bringing to mind one of my favorite executive lines, "I don't get ulcers—I give 'em." For the word "ulcers" I could substitute "chronic colitis," a personal specialty). We all know that workaday terror and stress is a superb motivational force, not to mention being pure pleasure to inspire.

Yet what can you do about the mental and health issues of these people over which you have had no direct influence? In other words, what do you do when underlings bring their physical and mental problems—*problems that you didn't cause*—into the workplace?

These little extras often come with the package, you know. You'll often find that these people have had physical and emotional difficulties before they were employed by you, and will have them after—although it is hard to believe that such a simple, basic organism as a salaried employee could contain such complicated disorders. But I've learned, often to my dismay, that they do.

DEALING WITH EMPLOYEES' PHYSICAL AND MENTAL DISORDERS

Obviously, you were not put on this earth to help people. But you do need to do something when their troubles begin to interfere with your business.

In this chapter I'll run through a catalog of what I've encountered in this area. Sadly, you *will* have to concern yourself personally with these issues. That is, until that golden day when business will be fully automated and computerized—and we can finally, totally rid ourselves of those damn nuisances and payroll-suckers, that is, our employees.

Let's Get Physical: Employees Who Get "Sick" and Don't Do Their Jobs

I'll begin with those employees who contract illnesses that cause them to lose time on the job. While it's true their illnesses might cause them some discomfort, what's far more important is the discomfort *you're* being caused. *You're paying them, and they're not working.*

That these people get sick isn't too surprising, considering their lifestyles. A typical meal for them is a double cheeseburger accompanied by fried onion rings, chased by one of those carbonated "citrus" drinks that have a drawing of a hillbilly on the can. They smoke generic-brand cigarettes, swill cheap beer, order well drinks from the bar, and of course ingest all manner of legal and illegal narcotics (which we'll address later). I've always considered it a miracle that these people's livers and colons don't leap out of their bodies and run screaming into the night.

Guess who ends up paying for their recklessness? That's right. You, the benevolent boss, who continues to dispense paychecks while people luxuriate and lounge in their sickbeds, having a good laugh at your expense.

I'd like to share, then, some of the methods I use to prevent employees' illnesses from interfering *too* much with the operation of my company.

Procedures to Help You Determine an Illness's Authenticity

The most important thing a responsible employer has to determine in regard to these critical employee health issues is whether or not these people are *faking it.*

Unfortunately, you can't trust your managers to adequately question employees who claim to be sick. Many managers today want to appear "sympathetic" and "caring"—and therefore don't get down to the dirty business of making sure that these people are *legitimately* ill.

I, on the other hand, will.

While I don't particularly enjoy this close contact with peons—especially ones who may be genuinely ill and thus packing all kinds of third-rate germs—I enjoy the thought of them taking a day off on my nickel even less.

Therefore I've instructed my managers to inform me whenever an inferior asks permission to go home due to illness. And I tell them I want to see these so-called sickies in my office *right now.*

Normally underlings who say they're sick will come into your office appearing haggard, pale, watery-eyed, with mouths ajar to suggest breathing difficulties. They may cough, sneeze, and even tremble, shudder, and shake to suggest fever and/or delirium.

But remember: These people are cunning—and some have the acting skills of an Olivier. It's amazing what makeup, eyedrops, and the like can do to make a perfectly healthy functionary appear sick as a dog.

The following is a sample examination/question-and-answer session you need to have with employees who would very much enjoy taking time off from performing their duties under the auspices of "illness"—more commonly known as "the slacker's friend."

The Executive Examination

The first question to ask in your office examination is a general one: "You're sick—or so you say. How exactly does this sickness manifest itself?"

In most cases the employee will reply with something along the lines of "Well, I got a sore throat, add a bad cough, I cad breathe, and I god a fever." Then they'll emit a piteous hack in an added grab for sympathy.

"Are both nostrils packed solid?"

"Uhh…yes."

"With what?…Come on, come on, I don't have all day."

"Uhh…congestchun. Mucus."

Do not take an employee at his or her word on the nostril question. Examine both nostrils with a penlight until you are satisfied both are fully congested with mucus. Then move on to the throat.

"Are you having trouble swallowing?"

"I cad swallow adythig. I cad eat adythig."

Here you should toss an M&M or a Junior Mint toward the employee. If the employee leaps up to catch the candy in his or her mouth, that's your tip-off you've got one Grade-A faker on your hands. If the candy merely bounces off the employee's head, continue your interrogation.

"Let's talk about your bowel movements."

"They're not too good."

"I'll need something a little more specific than 'They're not too good.'"

"I god diarrhea."

"I want to see a sample of this so-called diarrhea before you leave the building. How high is this fever you claim to have?"

"I took my temperature and it was 103."

"Was this temperature taken orally or anally?"

"Orally."

"When you bring in your diarrhea you'll take your temperature again, in my presence....Have you taken any aspirin, cough syrup, lozenges, or other over-the-counter preparations within the last four hours to relieve your symptoms?"

"I took 'em all."

"And they didn't relieve your symptoms adequately enough for you to feel you could continue performing your duties as you are being paid to do?"

"No, they didn't do ady good ad all."

After examining the employee's bowel movement sample and thermometer reading to your satisfaction, you should then—*and only then*—authorize the employee to leave the premises.

(*Note:* Be sure to inform your payroll department that any hours a sick employee spent "working" while ill counts against his or her quota for sick days. The hours may have been spent *at* the workplace, but certainly were not of any use to you. These people are even more worthless when they're sick.)

If an employee's illness is more serious, such as stroke, heart attack, seizure, or the like, it may be legally prudent to forgo the examination and let the employee take off work, especially if he or she is forced to exit the premises in an ambulance.

GOLDEN RULE: Employees who are too sick to come to work always *somehow* find the strength to lounge about in bed, drink fluids, suck on ice chips, and generally have a good old time of it—*while taking dollars out of your pocket.*

Postscript: Dealing with Hospitalized Employees

I have a large supply of get-well cards, which I bought in bulk in 1979 for $11 out of the trunk of a car, that I send to hospitalized employees.

On the front is a humorous drawing of a chicken in a coat and tie working at a desk. Inscribed inside are the words "Get Well Soon, Mr./Ms._____[here I have my secretary insert the name of the hospitalized employee]. You Never Know Who Might Take Over Your Position in Your Absence."

I then initial the card, date it, and get it notarized in case these people make some later courtroom claim that "My boss never even sent me a card when I was in the hospital." Sick or well, these people *will* try to paint you as a heartless rat. Believe me, I know.

Postscript II: Dealing with Dead Employees

Them you don't have to worry about. Do be sure, though, to get their work areas and desks cleared out quickly of any remaining traces of their employment to ensure the deceased don't take on "martyr" status in the minds of surviving employees. Again, believe me—I know.

Some Words on Your Company's Health Insurance Plan

During these dark days of employee "empowerment" the tide has turned so that your company practically *has* to supply some sort of group health insurance plan. There is no law dictating this *per se*, but pressure to do so from several corners is all-pervasive and insidious. You've fought this tide for years, and you've done your best to avoid getting swept up in it. But it's time to give up the ghost.

This is the cold, hard fact: *You are going to have to help pay for these people's health insurance.*

Twenty-five years ago, if you told me I'd make this statement—in print yet—I would have thought you were insane. As a matter of fact, I would have informed federal authorities that I suspected you of communist activities, because this was the kind of talk that I consider to be completely un-American. The thought of paying even an infinitesimal percentage of a perfect stranger's medical treatment, just because he or she happens to be in your employ, is absolutely outrageous.

But here's cheering news: Your company's health insurance plan doesn't have to be a very good one. Company health insurance plans that aren't very good also aren't very expensive.

Our company has hooked up with an excellent carrier, Fine 'n' Dandy Health Care Coverage, out of Needles, California, which costs us just pennies a day.

Of course the benefits of this outfit may not be the most advantageous to our employees: a co-pay of 95 percent (patient) to 5 percent (carrier) for office visits, outpatient treatment, and lab work; a somewhat steep $150,000 deductible for hospital stays (but which effectively prevents these people from lounging for days on end in a cozy hospital room for every little tumor that pops up); a list of primary care physicians whose licenses are currently under review by the state medical board; and a dental plan that provides patients access to selected inmates from a nearby institution for the criminally insane who have shown, as the warden of that institution puts it, "a certain flair for mouth and teeth work."

These people kicked and screamed for a group health plan, so we gave one to them. And on our end, we generously kick in 9 percent of the premium costs. During the last fiscal year, I'd estimate that the *total* cost to our company for our health insurance coverage was only in the very, very low four figures.

I can handle that.

But I still don't like it.

Drug Abuse, Personal and Family Problems, Mental Illness, and Other Inconveniences to Your Business

Not every problem an underling has can be tied to germs, bugs, or various diseases. They can get themselves into hot water very nicely on their own, thank you, without any help from physical or organic sources.

I'll start with the area of drug abuse, a problem that, as we all know, started in the hippie era of the '60s.

Drones on Drugs

If you suspect an employee is flying high on illicit drugs and narcotics, of course your first (and best) instinct is to turn him or her in to the proper authorities for vigorous prosecution and then, one would hope, a long period of incarceration.

Once again, to sing that tired old refrain, everything is more *complicated* these days.

Even without all the potential lawsuits and legal actions—not to mention embarrassing scenes like indignant denials or the underling promising "I swear I'll get off the stuff, I'm begging you to give me another chance, I'll make good, I promise" blah blah, yak yak—dealing with drug-addled employees is always problematic.

Remember, before you can do anything, you gotta catch 'em at it.

Drug Testing

We've instituted a drug-testing program at our company, but, as with every company policy I've initiated, employees always find a way to get around it.

We did monthly testing, and the vast majority of our employees "passed," but I had my suspicions. I found it hard to believe that with the way these people behaved they weren't doing *some* kind of drugs.

All the signs were there: complaints of being "tired," mumbling, nervousness, perspiring, yawning, slumping in chairs—all, of course, while they were being paid by me to *work*. Uppers, downers, morphine, cocaine, opium, heroin—who knew what they were on?

So I rigged catch basins in the company's toilets and urinals to collect samples of these people's urine every time they went to the lavatory. Of course, my suspicions were correct: *We found traces of alcohol and marijuana in quite a few of our employees' urine.* (We're dealing with a nasty little court case concerning this matter at present, but my attorneys tell me that urine is not necessarily constitutionally protected.)

What did we do with all these druggies and dopers?

Let's look at a specific case. We'll call him Raymond.

It seems our little friend Raymond had traces of alcohol in his urine.

Confronting the Drug-Addicted Employee

I confronted Raymond with our findings. Raymond did the indignant shtick at first, then went straight into the denial mode. It was a classic case.

I have a transcript of our conversation, which will be useful in demonstrating how these people try to evade responsibility for their actions—and how *you* have to handle it.

ME: Raymond, we found traces of alcohol in your urine. What do you have to say for yourself?

RAYMOND: You can't test me without my permission. It's illegal.

ME: We'll see about the legalities of the matter later. The fact is, we've got a serious problem on our hands.

RAYMOND: I've got no problem.

ME: Raymond, there was *alcohol*…in your *urine*. I'm not about to have a bunch of drunks lurching around this office.

RAYMOND: Sir, *I do not drink.* I drank two glasses of champagne at my son's wedding last weekend, which might explain the traces in the urine. Beyond that I haven't even had a single sip of beer since high school.

ME: Raymond, you're an *alcoholic.* I want you to get into a twelve-step program. By the way, that's not covered by Fine 'n' Dandy, so don't even ask.

RAYMOND: Sir—

ME: That will be all, Raymond.

You might say, You were pretty easy on that drunken bum. You should have kicked his butt right out the door.

Well, I could have—then spent hours and dollars training someone to replace him. But now I have Raymond over a barrel. When Raymond wants something from me that will cost me money, such as a leave or a raise, I can always say, "Raymond, I cannot in good conscience reward an alcoholic. That would be enabling you."

These people won't put themselves in treatment programs, because that would be admitting they have a problem.

So you have to help them yourself, by not caving in on their every demand for higher wages, cost-of-living increases, improved benefits, etc. Anytime an employee who has tested positive on my involuntary lavatory urine test comes to me for more money, I tell him or her, "You get this drug thing straightened out, then we'll talk." They leave my office shaking their heads. Very few of them return. They know I've got my eye on their urine.

Drug addiction is a tragic waste of people and resources. You might as well work it to your advantage.

Personal and Family Problems
We all enjoyed the little story about Dave at the beginning of this chapter. But his case is not an uncommon one.

Too often you'll find that your employees' performance suffers when they've got troubling personal or family situations on their "minds." Some of these problems, be they marital, family, or sexual, can seriously hamper these people. Then you've got a miserable and nonproductive worker on your hands rather than the ideal of a miserable and productive one.

The best way to show you how to deal with these sorts of problems is for me to briefly run through some of what I've encountered and demonstrate how I handled them. In all of these cases, the employee's performance had dipped so far below an acceptable level that I considered it my duty to intervene.

My intervention nipped these situations right in the bud. Afterward, these employees seemed to be more focused than ever, and worked in a kind of frenzy—almost as if they were being driven by some unspeakable rage.

Whatever. *Something* shoved their lazy noses back against the grindstone. That's all I care about.

(1) *A functionary with romantic problems.* Susan was still deeply in love with her fiancé, who had broken up with her to take up with her good friend. For weeks, in shock, Susan sat at her desk staring dully off into space, doing a stellar imitation of a zombie. Finally I brought her into my office.

"Susan," I said, "I know you're going through a difficult time. I sympathize—*up to a point*. But the fact is you're not performing the duties I'm paying you to perform. We can't have that.

"My advice to you is to go to a local bar and pick up a

young 'dude' who can make you happy for a night. A little 'action' will do you a world of good. And don't hold back, Susan. No one ever takes a taxi to go nowhere. Give him a little of this, a little of that, a little of the other thing. Plus it never hurts to wear heels, Susan. Heels are good.

"It's not my usual policy to be so openly encouraging to employees who are loafing on my time, but you've been reasonably productive in the past and I decided to give you the courtesy.

"Now get back to work or I'll give you the heave-ho faster than that boyfriend of yours ever dreamed of doing."

(2) *A functionary with marital problems.* Matt's wife wanted a divorce. She said she couldn't bear to be around him. He disgusted her. She had kicked Matt out of the house and already begun proceedings.

Consequently, Matt operated in the office in a profoundly depressed—and *extremely* nonfunctional—state. On the rare occasion when Matt did do his job, he basically phoned it in.

I called him into my office.

"Matt," I said, "I know you're going through a difficult time. I sympathize—*up to a point.*

"But the fact is that millions of people get divorced every year. What are you, special? You're just another statistic in the legion of losers. Don't worry about it. Why not rent a villa in Rome, find some nice Italian hooker to play house with, and kick up your heels? I'm not saying do it now, but when you retire and you're off the clock here. And don't ask about the pension business again, I don't have any answers on that yet.

"Now get back to work."

(3) *A functionary with family problems.* Elaine had always been one of our best salespeople. But then her adolescent son began to get into trouble at school. She was always on the phone with the school's teachers and counselors, negotiating, pleading, and arguing to keep her son from being expelled. Elaine's sales didn't dip—they drowned.

In my office, I said to Elaine, "Elaine, I know you're going through a difficult time. I sympathize—*up to a point.*

"The fact is you're becoming a drain to the payroll. If your boy is going to end up a serial killer or in the penitentiary there's little you can do about it now, and I see no reason why sales should suffer.

"You know, your boy can learn a trade in the pen. But he has to choose his friends carefully. And you do what you have to do to get along in the 'joint.' If that means becoming somebody's 'bitch' then so be it. It's better than a shiv in the throat, let me tell you.

"I'm sorry, Elaine, but I can't spend an entire afternoon trying to cheer you up about this matter. Get back to work."

(4) *A functionary in a sexual crisis.* Howard was tormented by a sexual crisis. He wanted, more than anything in the world, to be a woman. So he'd drag around the office or sit for hours at his desk, looking wistfully at fashion magazines.

I called him into my office.

"Howard," I said, "I know you're going through a difficult time. I know that there is a woman inside you struggling to get out, and I can sympathize—*up to a point.*

"But Howard, when she does get out, I need you to know that *I'm not interested.* I suspect your primary reason for getting a sex change is so you can jump my bones because I'm the boss and you're turned on by power. And you know I'm not a homosexual, and you wouldn't have a chance with me as a man. But Howard, you don't have a chance with me as a woman.

"Because, Howard, you always have to remember: *You can change your sex and become a woman, but you can't change your sex and become an executive.*

"Now give up this foolish pipe dream of yours and get back to work. And go watch a pro football game to get yourself back to normal."

(5) *A functionary with a death in the family.* Louise's husband of twenty-six years passed away, and she was having real trouble coping, even weeks after his death. Louise was a senior manager, and her department was beginning to go down the tubes because she wasn't paying attention to the details her work required. It was as if she didn't care anymore.

I called her into my office.

"Louise," I said, "I know you're going through a difficult time, and I can sympathize—*up to a point.*

"But you have to realize nobody lives forever. Your husband—what *was* his name?...I could have *sworn* I knew his name. Ah, what the hell, it doesn't matter—he certainly wasn't going to live forever.

"You have to realize he's gone. And I'm not going to blow any smoke up your dress about there being a 'heaven' or some kind of afterlife. I don't believe in that crap. I believe after death there's nothing, *nada,* zippo, a huge emptiness. That's my philosophy about it.

"Who was his doctor, anyway? Some of these incompetents don't know their ass from second base and they end up shoving you right into the grave. Oh, you got him through Fine 'n' Dandy? I'm sure he was excellent, excellent. I'm sure your husband was about to cash in his chips anyway and there was nothing anybody could do.

"Louise, it's time to move on with your life. It doesn't do any good to dwell on it. As a matter of fact, get back to work."

ASSORTED HINTS

In the preceding chapters I've given you some guidelines to follow in your role as a massive executive. Certainly there are going to be many situations you'll run up against as Big Boss that I haven't addressed.

In this chapter, I will attempt to fill a few of those gaps.

I'm going to run through a miscellaneous list of some of the specific challenges you'll face day to day as boss, and offer hints on how you should deal with them.

What you need to remember most of all is that *you've got the power.*

If by this point I still have to remind you to *use* it, you're a hopeless case and ought to be reading something else. Maybe a fairy story about little woodland elves with pointy shoes "nourishing" and "empowering" each other. You know, the kind of story you find in other management books.

Of course, after all the happily-ever-afters, what these books don't tell you is that little woodland elves usually get eaten by wolves or end up in management support groups.

GOLDEN RULE: Unused power will always
come back to bite you on the ass. And if you don't use
your power your ass deserves to be bitten, and everything
else on your froggy little body, too.

ASSORTED HINTS: PERSONNEL MATTERS

Family Leave
You may have an occasion when a female employee will require
time off to "have a baby." You heard right. A salaried position
in your employ isn't enough for some women. They want
"more."

Now, the law provides that you *have* to give this time to
her, and pay her while she's slacking off. For up to six weeks.
Six *weeks!*

Of course this is outrageous. Of course she should be back
at her desk the next day. You know it, I know it. But the law
doesn't know it. So you have to accommodate, accommodate,
and accommodate. What else is new?

But your employee *does* have a say in when she comes back
to work. If she wanted to come back to the office the day after
giving birth, she could.

Sadly, most employees don't have this sense of responsibility.
They milk the newborn stage for everything it's worth, sitting
around at home having a big old time with their feet up "nursing" their babies themselves, when they could just as easily hire
a lackey—while you suffer in the office struggling to get their
share of the work done. Sometimes you're even forced to hire
temporary help.

Two people being paid, thanks to *one* baby!

Our friend Mr. Marx the commie is no doubt having himself a good chuckle right now.

What I do, then, with recently babied underlings is let them know in no uncertain terms that while giving birth may be commendable it has no place interfering with the business of my company. (I don't really believe it's commendable for most of these people—you'll find that the final results of their urge to procreate are usually extremely unsatisfactory—but these types of things can become sticky legal matters if you're not careful in how you phrase them.)

In some instances I will call the mother at home and ask how the baby is. In response to the usual reply of "Good," I'll then say, "I'm glad the child is doing well. Because your department isn't."

Sometimes these women will reply, "Oh, (s)he's so beautiful"—in reference to the baby, of course—and I'll respond, "Well, the infant may be 'beautiful,' but all I see is that work isn't getting done. And that's ugly. Very ugly."

If she says, "It's really a miracle," I'll respond with, "That I'm paying an employee who isn't working is the only miracle in evidence here."

The message? *Everything might be sunshine and lollipops for you there in newborn vacation land, but you're not doing what I am paying you to do. And that's not acceptable.*

Other ways I encourage new mothers to stop their lollygagging: mail them the "Get Well Soon, You Never Know Who Might Take Over Your Position in Your Absence" greeting cards; send them Get Back to Work spit-up bibs; have my larger "associates" visit their homes to stare at their babies; and on occasion I will send the infant a bottle of scotch to let the mother know that I think the child is now grown up sufficiently and that its mother can leave its side and *get the hell back to work.*

Shockingly, in many of these women's cases, their nurturing instincts toward their newborn babies override their loyalty to me. So they use up a good portion or all of their allotted six weeks.

Unfair? You bet it is.

You'll just have to rack one up for the hippies and wimps.

On-site Child Care

I've heard that some companies make provisions on site to care for their employees' preschoolers. They provide caregivers, nap mats, building blocks, toys, food, and other entertainments for the tots.

Uh...*that hasn't happened here.*

And if you're even considering it for your company, you can just put this book down right now and leave the room. The thought of you makes me want to vomit.

Vacation "Daze"

Often when I'm interviewing prospective employees, they will ask about the company's "paid vacation policy."

What colossal nerve. You're not even hired and you're talking about vacations? I'll tell you what. Take your vacation *right now.* Tell you what! Since I'm not going to hire you, feel free to take as long a vacation as you like. Vacation your way to hell!

Paid vacations are the most overrated "benefits" in the history of American business. These people work a year, then expect a certain number of days of paid vacation. That's some sweetheart deal.

For you, the disadvantages are obvious. But we've all mindlessly gone along with the program, all in the name of avoiding worker "burnout." As if there were a danger of that. These people don't generate enough of a flame to light a cigarette.

In my company I only give paid vacation days to those who have *made a commitment* to me. I believe that five years is an appropriate time frame for us even to begin considering paid vacation days for employees. Five years of work shows me that a person has been willing to give up to me 7 percent—an approximation, taking into account factors such as personnel turnover, early death, etc.—of his or her life span.

So, in our organization, an employee who has been a reasonably steady and productive worker for the minimum five years is given the option of coming before the Vacation Board and stating his or her case as to why he or she feels they deserve paid vacation days.

The Vacation Board consists of me and a recently disbarred and disgraced lawyer, a real bulldog I hired for precisely these sorts of situations.

Collins v. the Vacation Board

VACATION BOARD: Collins, what exactly makes you feel you deserve a paid vacation at this juncture?

COLLINS: Sir, I really need to take some time off to spend with my family. I've worked every day for five years, and I'll tell you, the stress has really been building. I need to get away.

VACATION BOARD (*looking through Collins's file*): I see you took off five days of work two years ago. Would you care to explain that?

COLLINS: Sir, I was taken to the hospital with acute appendicitis. There were complications, and I was life-flighted to another facility. Then I came back to the hospital and was put under observation for a few more days.

VACATION BOARD: All this has been documented?

COLLINS: Yes, I think you'll find it in my file there.

VACATION BOARD: I see....I also see you didn't deem it necessary to call the office and explain your absence at the time or tell us when you'd be back.

COLLINS: My wife called my supervisor and told her.

VACATION BOARD: Yes, and it says here your wife was in such hysterics no one could understand a word she was saying. We like to hear it from the employee personally, Collins. We don't care to hear about these matters second-hand. There was also no proof supplied to us that your illness was what you said it was. Where was this so-called appendix that was giving you such a problem? We require you to bring in *any* removed organs for our inspection—or did you think since it was "just an appendix," we wouldn't want to see it? Did you think that an appendix was too piddling an organ for us to bother with? Because we assure you, that is not the case. All removed organs are equal before our eyes.

COLLINS: Sir—

VACATION BOARD: Application for vacation denied. Perhaps during your next "medical emergency," you'll be good enough to let us know exactly when you plan on sauntering back into the office. We'll see you in another five years if you care to try again. Now get back to work.

As you can see, we give our workers fair hearings, and sometimes we *do* award vacation days. We do require nonmanagement employees to stay in-state and leave their phone numbers so we can call them back in to work if necessary. For most of these people a vacation consists of two days of nonstop eating and television watching, so it doesn't matter.

I do remember one underling who didn't "like" this requirement and gave us a bogus phone number when he took

off for Florida. When he got back to the office after his unauthorized fun in the sun, he had a little surprise waiting for him:
a stranger working at his desk, and a pink slip in his mailbox.

Life's a beach, as various idiots say.

GOLDEN RULE: Human needs, dreams,
and desires are boulders blocking the river of your
cash flow. Dynamite them the hell out of there.

Amenities

*People wanna eat, let 'em go to a restaurant. I'm tryin' to run a
bidness here.*
— Lao Dung,
14th-century Chinese philosopher and merchant

I've learned through the years that it's often the small things
that are important. Time and time again you'll discover that it's
the little "extras" that mean so much to your employees. A
decent place to eat lunch, access to drinking water, convenient
parking—these and other amenities you supply as boss add up
to a pleasant and hospitable working environment.

That's why I don't like to supply these things. I'm running a
business, not a country club with all manner of chairs, water,
and other fripperies. You make it too comfortable for these people and believe me, they'll start treating your company like their
homes. Next thing you know they've got their shoes off, there's
a plastic bowl filled with cheese doodles on their desks, mud on
the floor, and their cats are using your In-basket as a litter box.

Sound good to you? I didn't think so.

Here are a few common workplace amenities—and how *you*
can live with them.

The Lunchroom: A Disaster Waiting to Happen

I am aware that some companies supply their employees with kitchens complete with cupboards, refrigerator, microwave, and sink, as well as a dining table surrounded by comfortable, cushioned chairs for mealtime convenience. Some organizations even *buy food* for these people. It wouldn't surprise me to hear that they cut the crusts off their sandwiches for them, or even give them little bendy straws for their soda pops.

Do I really have to explain why this is a bad idea? Do I really have to reiterate what I've been saying, in so many words, throughout this book?

These people are being paid to *work*. Not to smile. Not to talk. Not to laugh. Not to have a "career" or to "fulfill" themselves.

They're *certainly* not being paid to eat!

If you allow a kitchen/dining area to be a part of your office, you're sending a message to these people. You're sending the message that it's *okay* to eat.

While it is accepted business practice to give underlings time off to have lunch, this doesn't mean that lunch should be encouraged. If you put a comfortable eating facility in your office, lunch is *precisely* what you're encouraging. Not only that, you're encouraging snacks. Lunch and snacks—is that what your business is all about? What's next? Brunch? Wine and cheese tastings? Light suppers? Midnight raids on the fridge? Once they start there's no stopping them. These people will be picking their teeth while you and your company go straight down the toilet. They don't care—as long as they get their precious "chow."

In my company, I have designated a former janitor's closet as the "lunchroom." Inside are a wobbly card table and four splintery wooden chairs. There is a utility sink, so underlings can wash any plates that they have brought from home. (We dilute the dishwashing liquid because people always, *always* use more soap than they need to get the job done. Did you know that, if given the opportunity, they'll squeeze as much liquid onto their dishes as they squeeze lighter fluid onto their barbecue coals? That's the way these people live.)

Hanging from the ceiling in this "lunchroom" is a lone lightbulb, frosted an unappetizing brownish green, which makes any food take on a sickening hue. Along the floorboards are rat and mouse traps, and on the walls are posters with the messages:

DON'T MAKE A PIG OF YOURSELF

ROACH CROSSING

**FOODS CONTAINING FAT AND SODIUM
MAY CAUSE CANCER OF THE ANUS**

ALMOST DONE EATING? TIME'S RUNNING OUT

**PLEASE DISPOSE OF ANY RATS OR MICE
YOU SEE CAUGHT IN TRAPS**

WATCH YOUR TIME!

**SQUEEZE THE DISHWASHING DETERGENT BOTTLE FOR A
COUNT OF ONE ONLY WHILE WASHING YOUR DISH**

and of course

GET BACK TO WORK

Watercoolers

As we discussed in an earlier chapter, people will always take advantage of your generosity in giving them a supply of fresh, pure water. And, as I said, in a fit of pique I removed the watercooler. Ultimately, however, I did put it back after hearing far too much water whining. You'd think these people needed it to live the way they carried on.

However, I saw no reason to pay for water twice. So to refill the "mountain spring water" jugs, we merely siphon water from the toilets. It's economical, and provides a double dose of chlorine, a necessary nutrient.

Coffeemakers: No Problemo

Many of my employees like to drink coffee to give them a boost during the day. Their cup of Yuban or Chock Full o' Nuts certainly gives them an energy "buzz" that often *does* translate into more work getting done. And you can be sure I applaud heartily any deviation from their usual torpor.

So I supply coffeemakers throughout the office, to encourage that wondrous energy generated by caffeine. My associate Bruno makes it and crumbles caffeine tablets, diet pills, and even amphetamines into the roast to really give these people a turbo charge.

I also tell my employees we use our "mountain spring water" for that *perfectly* brewed cup of coffee.

Vending Machines

Although the idea of vending machines dispensing soda, snack cakes, potato chips, candy bars, and the like on my premises is anathema to me, I was convinced by a tattooed acquaintance from a local vending company that this would be a "healthy" idea for my company and, more critically, for me.

So at present we have two vending machines in the bottom floor of our building. I've asked Bruno to "find his way" into the machines and crumble all the chips, crackers, and cookies; thumb-crush the peanut butter cups; remove crucial numbers of Milk Duds and M&M's from their packages, leaving at the most only four or five Duds or M's; make sure the honey buns and other pastries are well expired; and shake up all the cans of soda.

There's nothing like killing two birds with one stone. I deprive my vending "friend" of any income from his machines in my building and, most important, I deprive my functionaries of snacks.

Convenient Parking

Only my senior managers are permitted to park in the lot adjacent to the building—one of the perks of the job. No, they can't park on the carpeted area, as I do, and they aren't permitted to park under the dome I have installed over my space during the winter, and I don't want them with me on the private People Mover that takes me to my entrance, but they are well within shouting distance of the front door.

As for the rest of the employees, there is a yearly raffle to determine who gets to park in the "near" lot. The near lot is approximately—well, you remember the scene in *The Wizard of Oz* when Dorothy and her ineffectual little chums get their first glimpse of the Emerald City? The near lot, in relation to our building, is approximately equidistant to the Dorothy aggregation in relation to the Emerald City. Functionaries can clearly *see* the building. Once they have the building in sight, I'm not concerned with the problems they might encounter in getting to it.

And do they ever put on a big show of panting and gasping for breath when they do arrive! As if walking a piddling two and a half miles was crossing the Gobi Desert.

As for the rest, they'd better find a quicker way to get to the office from the so-called far lot, or there are going be a lot of people driving to the unemployment office. Ample parking is available there.

◻

OVERHEAD, OFFICE SUPPLIES, MISCELLANEOUS TIPS, AND DOS AND DON'TS

If salaried employees were meant to be comfortable, the Lord would have put chaise lounges in their mothers' wombs.
—Ray Hunt, President and CEO, Goering Industries

In this section, I'd like to bang out a series of quick and dirty hits on a potpourri of topics.

Just remember the overriding theme: *Spend as little money as humanly possible.* There's nothing quite so rewarding to an executive as looking out over a working office—and knowing that he or she didn't spend diddly on any of the stuff in it.

Office Furniture

Some concern themselves with *ergonomics.* I, of course, concern myself with *economics.*

I get office chairs from Goodwill or other charitable organizations. Most of these are of the odd diner set, or kitchenette, variety, usually dating from the '50s or early '60s. Employees are permitted, after proper authorization, to drape layers of paper toweling over the wooden backs of some of these chairs if the varnish has chipped away. They are also permitted to cover any holes in vinylette seats with duct tape.

I have one designated lackey, a junior manager who is serving hard time on my shit list, to scout neighborhood lawns for discarded planks, boards, tabletops, etc., as well as construction sites for bricks he can "borrow" on which to set these flat planes. Voilà! The functionary's desk.

Cardboard boxes that can be purchased at any discount mart serve perfectly well as drawers and storage utilities. Junior managers are permitted to Magic Marker their names on their boxes; senior managers are permitted to decorate their boxes in

a tasteful manner, such as with blue or red ribbons or paste-on silver stars.

Computers

Our computers are from Cut Rate Technologies, out of Dallas, Texas, and did I get a deal on them. The whiners here complain that they're constantly crashing and losing data, they have to whack the side of the monitors to get the cursor moving, and there's a funny smell coming out of many of the machines, but at these prices, who cares?

I also take full advantage of the black market to access hardware, software, and supplies. Buying obsolete or even dangerous hardware can provide huge savings.

Note: Do not buy Cut Rate's 1200SXZ computer: We had a real problem with fireballs shooting out of that machine. The hospitalization costs far outweighed the savings.

A Few Software Tips

A particularly inexpensive software package for spreadsheets is Blank Page from SofteeTex, which presents a gray screen that, upon being printed out, provides a blank page. Then, of course, your accountant can get busy with his or her pencil and ruler and construct a spreadsheet—*just as he or she was hired to do.* Bonus: This application takes no memory to run.

Another inexpensive graphic package from Softee is Invisible Graphix, again supplying a blank printout; from CompuPuds comes Lo-Ball Word Processing, with its cost-busting 18-Letter Alphabet; and from Pit Bull Systems comes Crime and Punishment software, which senses when users have been slacking off and emits powerful radiation and blinding lights to repeat offenders.

Not to mention we got a superb deal on "Get Back to Work *Now!*" screen savers from Niggling Inc.

Pencils, Pens, Notepads, Calendars, Address Books
Create such difficulty for your employees in obtaining these kinds of small items from you that ultimately, in exasperation, they'll go out and pay for them themselves.

A dollar here and a dollar there adds up!

On Another Note: Mood Music
I pipe in marches, martial music, and African drumming to get the drones to labor to a military beat. Barely audible, but insistent, the music burrows into the depths of these people's souls:

Do your work, get it done, now begin again....Do your work, get it done, now begin again....Do your work, get it done, now begin again....Do your work, get it done, now begin again....

Clocks
Once or twice a week, near the end of the day, I set them back forty-five minutes. You'd be surprised at how effective this is. By the time employees get wise, they've worked twenty-five hours overtime—for free.

Dos and Don'ts
Do keep putting off those meetings with your people about 401(k) or other retirement plans. These plans *cost you money.*

Do award workers a certificate, personally signed by you, upon their retirement. You can find some hippie art student willing to do the calligraphy for peanuts.

Don't profit-share.

Do instruct Security to escort an employee out of the office once a month to serve as an example to the others.

Don't profit-share.

Don't give out year-end bonuses unless you have a carefully thought out plan to get the money back in one way or another.

Do plant pornography in troublesome employees' desks.

Do question an employee's loyalty if he or she wonders why there are no year-end bonuses.

Don't hesitate to deal with the so-called criminal element of your community. They can save you money!

Do get rid of any underling whose presence—for whatever reason—annoys you. You can always come up with a "valid" reason later. Life's too short!

Do lie about "not feeling well" before planned meetings about 401(k) or retirement plans. The very idea *does* make you sick, doesn't it?

Don't allow *any* underling to question you in public without exacting your pound of flesh later on.

Do cultivate a positive image with the media in your town. They'll never catch on.

Don't even *think* about letting those union bastards get a foot in the door. Once they're in, you're history.

Don't profit-share.

MY DAY

All right. So far we've talked about establishing your executive persona, solidifying your power, motivating and punishing employees, as well as taking a proactive approach to their problems so they don't become yours.

Now I'd like to take you along with me, hour by hour, on one of my typical days.

On September 12, 1996, I recorded in a journal and on audiotape everything I did and everyone I spoke to, expressly for this book.

This log will give you the opportunity to see how what I've discussed in previous chapters is put into action by a *real-life* executive.

I trust you will find it instructive.

7 A.M. I awoke. Jake brought me my coffee, papaya juice, toast, marmalade, and soft-boiled egg. I dismissed him from the room and read the newspaper. More trouble in one of those Third World countries. Quelle surprise. They need an American executive over there to instill a little discipline and maybe they wouldn't be hitting each other over the heads with sticks when they get hungry.

Then again, we should think about opening a factory over there—labor could be even cheaper than in China or Honduras. Look into this.

7:45 A.M. Took a shower. Can *still* smell lingering cologne from Jansen in Marketing! These people are coming far too close to me—Jansen was consistently violating the three-foot boundary. Possible homosexual? Have V. investigate.

8:15 A.M. Drove Lexus to office. A Plymouth Horizon tried to cut me off. She won't try *that* again. Boy, those things just crumple up. Made note to call attorney and insurance company and make quick settlement to keep her quiet. Three grand should do it (take out of office expenses).

8:30 A.M. Arrived at office and met by Bendix and Rogers, who both fell all over themselves to say good morning. Brushed them off. Not today, ass kissers. Liston started to say something, but I pushed him out of the way.

People stared at my clothes again as I walked by. Eat your hearts out. You'll never wear anything like this. They wouldn't even let people like you in the shop. Of course, you have to fly in a jet to even get to *my* tailor. He's in London, you know. That's in England. It's part of Europe. Big ocean you have to cross and everything? Ring a bell? Idiots.

Went over to Brown's terminal, turned it on, logged on using her password, and deleted all the files from her hard drive. A mole told me she had been updating her résumé on one of the files, so I nuked them all.

Not on my equipment, dear.

8:45 A.M. Donna gave me my messages, and I got a call from Richards at Penco. Shipments late again! Put blame on Howell, even though he's still in hospital. These slackers will put me out of business yet.

And how long do I have to put up with all this "bypass"

crap from this Howell character? Get word to him he better get his ass back in the office *now* (have Donna send card).

9–9:45 A.M. Reviewed and signed off on various written requests and memos. "No." "Rejected." "Tell him to go f_ _ _ himself." "No no no no no." "Disapproved." "Tell her it's not in the budget and maybe we can give her one next year (ha ha)." "Stonewall it." "Ain't no way." "Check his urine." "I want her gone by Christmas." "Handle it—that's what I'm paying you for." "Not in budget." "If she doesn't turn it around you tell her she's history." "Nix on that." "N-O spells no."

Got a call from Lewis about M.'s harassment case. Tells me "this one might not go away so easily." Great. This is the thanks you get for employing people. What do I expect.

10–11 A.M. Staff meeting. Rogers's presentation on expansion to Indiana market, then Willis's on necessity of computer system upgrade. I ask Willis if we really need to upgrade, or is all this just a ploy so he and the rest of the geeks in the office can try out the latest computer games. His face turned beet red. Good.

Stared at Bell and made her fidget.

Pretended to track flight of imaginary bug during Carlton's comments. Thinks she's so smart. She's going to last about five minutes here, her and her big "ideas."

11 A.M. Talked to accountant on phone. Told him to relax, the state can damn well keep waiting for its precious tax payment. He says no. I said, "Then you better get creative," and hung up on him.

11:15 A.M. TV reporter and crew from Channel 6 here to interview me about market trends and how company is faring. Rented a few actors to come into the office, look admiringly at me, and ask me for advice. "My door is always open!" I called after them on-camera. You never know who might be watching—

a future juror in one of my court cases, maybe? But even *pretending* to say this makes my skin crawl.

11:30 A.M. Queered a job reference for Blauser. You quit this company and you want *me* to give *you* a reference? What chutzpah! You'll be lucky to get a job bagging groceries, you bum. Hey Blauser, paper or plastic? Ha ha ha! Go to hell!

11:40 A.M. Reviewed materials and pricing Willis gave me on this new computer system he's looking at. I am not paying these prices! Made a note to stall Willis and talk to V. about getting some software and chips from his little buddies in Yugoslavia.

Since when do these people need designer electronics? Their brains can barely get around crayons and drawing paper! And I'm going to pay this kind of money for the privilege of watching them spill convenience-store coffee and pastry crumbs on the keyboards? Willis must think I just fell off a turnip truck.

Is there a nice fat demotion and pay cut in Mr. Willis's future? I do believe there is!

11:50 A.M. My ex's lawyer called. Now *I'm* expected to pay for her last six years of psychotherapy! Whatever happened to personal responsibility? Well, I can always snip some salaries here and there or take it out of expenses. Anything to keep that lunatic out of my hair.

Noon. Peter prepared me a lunch of a small Caesar salad, lobster Newburg, steamed rice, and persimmon pudding. Call about ex's therapy upset me so I didn't feel like anything too fancy. Afterward, still upset, so decided not to leave scraps in bucket outside office door for underlings to pick through. I've done this a few times, so now, of course, they expect it. Surprise, surprise.

I'll take it home to King. My big doggy just wuvs his wobster!

1 P.M. I called Harris into my office to talk about her performance lately, or lack thereof. Seems Ms. H. has some serious
"financial problems" that are causing her a great deal of worry.
Told her I was sympathetic up to a point, etc., etc., but just
because she's got loan sharks banging on the door at all hours of
the night doesn't excuse her doing a distracted and subpar job. I
pointed out to her that this job was the only lifeline she had
and she'd damn well better shape up or I'd ship her out.

I felt very "up" after our conversation. There's nothing like giving a recalcitrant employee a reality check to get the juices flowing.

1:10 P.M. Got a call from one of those damn disease organizations asking if we'd cosponsor a 10K race to raise money for
diabetes research. I said to the woman, "Just tell them to watch
their sugar" and hung up on her. Are we supposed to take care
of *every* sickie in the world around here? When are these people
going to start pulling their own weight?

1:15 P.M. Gave Podner, our biggest competitor, a jingle.
Accused him of getting his trouble boys to sabotage our
Detroit-bound shipment. He said "I don't know a thing" about
the goods not arriving in one piece and as much as called me
crazy. Made note to talk to V. about arranging a little "accident"
with one of *their* trucks. There'll be cough syrup *all* over the
highway in southern Ohio, my friends!

1:30 P.M. Watched my secretly taped videos of functionaries
flushing items down the lavatory toilets. Noted who, what,
when, etc. Who do these people think they're dealing with,
Helen Keller?

Made notes to remove paper towels and dispensers from
lavatories after seeing people stuffing them in their pockets and
purses and taking them home to use as napkins or God knows
what. Of course *then* they'll demand air dryers. Sure, you'll get
air dryers—when hell freezes over.

Also: Remind V. to keep diluting soap. Just another luxury that's being abused. And have plumber reduce water pressure in faucets to a dribble, too. These people have to realize this isn't the Ritz.

1:50 P.M. Brought Kahn into my office, turned off the lights, put a baby spot on him, and accused him of spying for Podner. Well, wasn't he the indignant one! Made note to have him followed.

2 P.M. Reviewed materials from Might-E-Tite Security, which I'm thinking of hiring to protect my home. My current security company, Lok-M-Up, isn't doing the job. Last week I spotted a low-level employee—*one who'd only been hired two and a half years ago*—within 200 yards of my gate!

When I approached him and asked what he was doing in the neighborhood, he said he was "waiting for a friend." I thought: A "friend"—in this neighborhood? With *you?* There isn't a convenience store or a tacoria, the only things you or your friends could possibly be interested in, anywhere *near* here!

Maybe, just maybe, your "friend" is coming to help you snatch me, stuff me in that disgusting Pontiac you drive, take me to an abandoned shack outside of town, and then demand a pretty little ransom!

Lok-M-Up says they "can't just shoot" these people, but they don't even bother roughing them up to find out what they're up to. If I decide to go with Might-E-Tite then I'll have to get everyone's dossiers *back* from Lok-M-Up and then over to them. It's as delicate as changing your dentist, I'm telling you.

2:15 P.M. Had big scheduled meeting with senior managers in my office to discuss expanding our pension and retirement plans. Faked violent coughing fit and they eventually left, but before they did, I told them between hacks we'd "reschedule soon." Ha ha ha.

2:30 P.M. Took a call from a woman from Planet Earth First or some such thing telling me we weren't being "responsible" in terms of producing enough recyclable packaging. Put the phone down while this chatterbox prattled on, played a little solitaire, went to the bathroom, gargled, etc. Then got back on the horn and gave her the runaround.

Hey, I have an idea. Why don't these nonprofit environmental do-gooders and nutcases take all the money they're sucking from the government, hire some inner-city jokers at minimum wage to pick up all the garbage, and leave respectable businessmen alone. How would that be?

2:40 P.M. Called in Folsom from Accounting and asked her to give me a detailed description, in twenty-five words or less, of our cash flow the past three quarters. Of course she started by asking "In twenty-five words or less?" which, boom, is five words down already. Then she stuttered and stammered, using up even more, until I finally just booted her out of my office in disgust.

Oh, these people love their fancy titles, but when it comes to delivering the goods? *Disappear-o.*

2:45–3 P.M. Suki gave me my massage. Asked her to hum tunes from *The King and I* this time.

3 P.M. Inspected Gray's nostrils for mucus, then sent him back to work. These people must really think I was born yesterday.

3:10 P.M. A reporter from the *Daily* called and asked me to comment on a group of protesters in wheelchairs outside one of our stores, whining about lack of "access." Gave him the usual "we're working on it" baloney and hung up. These cripples and wheelchair jockeys are going to drive me absolutely bananas!

First we paint wheelchairs in a few parking spots in our lots—and then they bitch because they're "at the far end of the lot"! Then we move them by the doors—and they gripe about the steps! We cave in and put up a few ramps, and then they moan about the door handles being too hard to reach! Am I supposed to take care of *everybody* around here?

3:25 P.M. Had Donna hold calls, put on headphones, and listened to Wagner. Those were the good old days.

3:45 P.M. Interviewed a young man named Griggs who's applying for a job in Sales. He passed the Staring, Insult, and the Shoulder Grip Tests in acceptable fashion, but then I pretended to call one of his references in his presence. That's where our friend Mr. Griggs slipped up.

"So, Ben, what would you say are Griggs's main weaknesses as an employee or otherwise?" I said to the dead phone. "Unh-huh...yesss...oh, really? Yes, he does look somewhat evasive to me, too—what do *you* think he's running from? Himself?...Hmm, that's interesting.

"Did you check his urine periodically?...You can't prove anything unless it shows up in the tests. Well, he might just have been *born* with beady eyes. No, his skin doesn't appear unusually yellow, but the light's a little soft in here....Yesss...unh-huh...oh, of course, it's *terrible*. It's a terrific drain on business and on the country, definitely. Oh, yes, they ought to be lined up and shot, I agree completely.

"No, he hasn't indicated any particular preference of that nature to *me,* but he's only been here a few minutes. There were complaints in the bathrooms? *That's* not good. The vice squad, huh? Really! Well, it's not like we have a casino in the office, so he can't get into any trouble on *that* count. Ha ha ha, that's funny....All right, thank you, Ben. I'll meet you in the clubhouse at seven. *Ciao.* "

My goodness, was Mr. Griggs worked up after my little pretend conversation with his former employer!

"What was he telling you?" he demanded.

"Oh, a little of this, a little of that, a little of the other thing," I said nonchalantly. "Nothing to worry about."

"None of that, none of it, is true," Griggs said. "I don't know what he was telling you....I don't have any sort of record of—what was he telling you?"

We danced around in like manner for a few minutes, until finally Griggs broke down and admitted he did have a "minor" gambling problem "back in college" but he hadn't "bet on any games in years" and that he had "paid back every penny." He also confessed to being "a bit of a pot smoker" in his younger years. I think if we'd kept talking he would have eventually confessed to being the Unabomber. These people get so flustered!

Of course I put him in the reject pile. Who wants some drug-addicted compulsive gambler on the payroll?

4 P.M. Read some mail. Here's a letter from a student at a local high school, asking me to speak to her Economics class. My speaking fee is $5,000, dear. Think you can get the school district to pony that up? No? Then go pound sand.

Here's a request from a local charity asking me to be a judge for a costume contest at an upcoming benefit ball. My costume-contest judging fee is $3,500. Think you can pony that up? Then see above.

Here's a sweepstakes form from *Reader's Digest.* Told Donna to send it back and make sure the stickers are properly affixed. I am not going to tolerate getting chiseled out of an extra fifty grand just because my secretary was too stupid to put the right sticker on the entry form. It's the *round* one, dammit!...Do I have to do everything around here?

Well, here's a letter from two exes back. She writes, "When I married you, I didn't have a clue as to what you were. Now that I'm forced to take up half my time pursuing you through

the courts to get you to pay your measly amount of child support—pocket change to you—I find it impossible to believe
that I could ever, *ever* have spent a single solitary minute with
you, much less marry you. You are the lowest of the low, a
worm, scum, slime. I must tell you, I tremble in revulsion at
the very thought of you. Even fourteen years after the fact, I'm
still astounded at my own stupidity." Hey, you said it, I didn't.

Here's another threatening letter about my back taxes from
the feds. Maybe I'll send *you* a payment, my friend, when you
send *me* that itemized list I keep asking for of where exactly this
money is going! Why can't they leave honest businessmen
alone?

Here's one that cheered me up: a note from one of my
attorneys telling me that D. is dropping his wrongful termination suit against me. It hurt me that my own mentor would
bring that kind of action against me. Well, he always was a big
baby.

Here's promotional material from one of those motivational
speakers, a marketing guru. Ooh, he says he will teach my sales
people to "empower" customers to "improve" their lives (i.e.,
convince them to buy what they're selling).

That's funny. That's very similar to what *I* tell my sales people: "Empower" your way to your quota or I'll "impede" your
paycheck. I guess I'm a motivational speaker, too.

Here's a letter from an ex-employee who's now working out
of state, and doing very well indeed. "I think the best thing
about working for you," she writes, "is that now I can see clearly that everything you did was exactly the opposite of the way it
should be done. It took a few years for me to catch on because
you were so sneaky, but you must know the increasing turnover
at _____ is due to your presence and your presence alone.

"You've been getting away with it because profits have been

up—temporarily, I believe—but sooner or later it's going to catch up with you. Exploiting and underpaying people and making them run around in circles at your whim is not going to work in the long term.

"Please, please look to your conscience and consider taking an early retirement rather than running the company into the ground. There are many qualified people there, friends of mine, who could manage the business until a suitable replacement is found. You could get a fantastic retirement package, I know, and come out with your reputation somewhat intact. I'm afraid if you continue this course the results could be catastrophic for both you and the company.

"Sincerely and respectfully," etc. etc.

Hmm, very interesting idea. Food for thought. And she sounds genuinely concerned, though she always was quite the Goody Two-Shoes. Think I'll just take a peek at her file and see exactly who these "friends" of hers might be.

4:45 P.M. Looked at my Lexus in the executive parking lot through power binoculars. I saw a little smudge of grease on the rear passenger window the other day, which leads me to believe that *someone* is touching my car. I paid a nice chunk of change for that alarm system, and if people are touching my car and I don't hear that very expensive alarm go off, then something is terribly wrong with this picture. What if company functionaries are eating greasy food at lunch and then walking over to my car and touching it? What good is owning a luxury automobile if people are constantly rubbing their dirty fingers on it? *Where the hell is Security?*

4:50 P.M. Smoked a cigar and looked at myself in the oak-framed mirror as I did so. I must say I was enormously touched.

5:10 P.M. Rosenzweig came into the office to put another half-hour of work on my portrait. I told him to put more highlights in my eyes, and paint in more of those angels fluttering around my head and adoring me. For what I'm paying, I should get more angels.

Also told him to make one of them black. Never let it be said we're not inclusive here.

6:15 P.M. Quitting time. Walked out to the Lexus and kept my palm placed against my jacket lapel, so everyone could see that I had instant access to the Old Persuader.

Punched in my security code, settled into the plush leather, put Wagner on the CD player, put her in gear, and cut off some functionary's Cherokee in the parking lot.

Made a note of the Cherokee's license plate. Next time, make no mistake, he *will* wait for me to go first. Punk.

How Real Leaders Talk

As you progress in your role as leader, you'll find that you're uttering particular phrases and statements to inferiors again and again.

If you're *not* a real leader, these phrases and statements might include: "Thank you," "Terrific job," "You'll find a nice extra in your paycheck this month," "Let's talk about it," "Let's get your input on this," "We're behind you a hundred and ten percent," "My door is always open," "I have complete confidence in you," "This sounds like a terrific opportunity but we'll sure miss you," "Profit-sharing is the way to go," and "Let's talk about ideas for retirement plans for our people."

However, if you *are* a real leader, they'll include:

"I'LL GIVE YOU SOMETHING TO CRY ABOUT."

"IT'S NOT HEALTHY TO DISAPPOINT ME."

"NOBODY ASKED YOU."

"YOU DON'T EXIST."

"YOU'LL DO BETTER TO MIND YOUR P'S AND Q'S."

"SHUT THE F_ _ _ UP."

"WHEN HELL FREEZES OVER."

"WHEN MONKEYS FLY OUT MY BUTT."

"OUT OF MY WAY, SMALL FRY."

"WHO THE HELL ARE YOU?"

"THIS ISN'T YOUR CONCERN. GET OUT AND SHUT THE GODDAMN DOOR BEHIND YOU."

"I'M NOT PAYING YOU TO SIT THERE LIKE A DEAD RAT."

"LOOK ALIVE, FOR GOD'S SAKE."

"HELLO IN THERE! ANYBODY HOME?"

"YOU DON'T 'TRY,' YOU DO IT."

"CLEAN OUT YOUR EARS, GODDAMIT! I DON'T LIKE TO CHEW MY CABBAGE TWICE."

"YOU SASSING ME?"

"WAAH, BOO HOO HOO."

"WHO THE HELL GAVE YOU THAT HAIRCUT?"

"WHO THE HELL SOLD YOU THOSE CLOTHES?"

"YOU LOOK LIKE SOMETHING THE CAT DRAGGED IN."

"YOU GET YOUR ASS IN HERE OR I'LL REALLY MAKE YOU SICK."

"YOU DRINK MORE MOUNTAIN WATER THAN A DAMN MOOSE. LEAVE A LITTLE FOR THE REST OF US."

"NOT ON MY TIME."

"I'M NOT PAYING YOU TO EAT."

"I'M NOT PAYING YOU TO SMILE."

"I'M NOT PAYING YOU TO CHAT WITH EACH OTHER."

"I'M NOT PAYING YOU TO LOOK AT EACH OTHER."

"I'M NOT PAYING YOU TO STARE OUT INTO SPACE."

"Planning on doing some work today for a change?"

"News flash: I'm in charge here."

"What is this, a goddamn state fair? Throw that bag of nuts out."

"Am I supposed to thank you for doing your job?"

"Give me that and get out."

"You earn your benefits around here, my friend."

"Vacation! Who the hell told you you were due for a vacation?"

"Taking a week's vacation, eh? A lot can happen in a week."

"The last person who screwed with me is living in a cardboard box out on the street."

"The last person who tried blowing the whistle on me ended up being humiliated by Mike Wallace on 60 Minutes."

"You were born to be downsized."

"I don't have time to hear about your 'problems,' I've got a business to run."

"Oh, you're 'concerned,' huh? Well, boo hoo hoo."

"Don't whine to me about 'right' and 'wrong,' I've got a business to run."

"Unacceptable. Do it over."

"Because I say so, that's why."

"Now I've got a question: How'd you like me to can your ass?"

"Has anyone ever told you that you're a complete idiot?"

"I'll kill you."

"You couldn't take five steps without screwing up."

"I find it extraordinary that a lunkhead like you is actually employed."

"Are you on narcotics?"

"Are you drunk or just stupid?"

"This is what they taught you in college?"

"One more like you and we'll be out of business in no time."

"That fancy degree of yours isn't much help now, is it?"

"You don't have to know why, college boy—JUST DO IT."

"No, it isn't that your work is unacceptable, it's that you are."

"I think it's time you got on with your life's work."

"Soon you're going to be nothing more than a bad memory."

"The end is near, my friend."

"Three guesses as to why I called you in here."

"Let me begin by saying the raise thing isn't going to happen."

"It's my distinct pleasure to inform you that you're fired."

"You're history. Now get out."

"You leave your keys at the reception area. Don't make us come after you with a pack of dogs."

"Our legal department will chew you up and spit you out because they like it. CAPISH?"

"The 'joint' is no place to be this time of year."

"Ms. Johnson, call Security. And see if you can hold him down in the meantime."

"NOW PUT THAT DOWN...PUT THAT DOWN."

"IF I KNEW YOU FELT THAT STRONGLY ABOUT THIS ISSUE, WE
COULD HAVE TALKED. NOW <u>PUT THAT DOWN</u>."

"TELL THEM TO BRING ALONG THE SWAT TEAM. AND USE MY
NAME."

BONUS SECTION: HOW THE WANNABE LEADER SHOULD TALK TO HIS OR HER SUPERIORS

"YOU HANDLED THAT SITUATION MAGNIFICENTLY."

"YOUR OUTFITS ALWAYS MATCH SO PERFECTLY. IT'S REALLY
QUITE UNCANNY."

"WHERE DID YOU GET THAT MARVELOUS TIE?...WAIT, I WANT
TO WRITE THIS DOWN."

"THIS IS HOW DWIGHT EISENHOWER GOT HIS START. BUT YOU
HAVE LOTS MORE HAIR."

"THIS IS HOW MARGARET THATCHER GOT HER START. BUT
YOU'RE SO MUCH MORE ATTRACTIVE."

"THE WAY YOU SQUISHED THAT PUNK INTO A GELATINOUS
PASTE WAS PURE POETRY."

"WOULD IT EMBARRASS YOU IF I TOLD YOU THAT YOU WERE MY
IDOL?"

"THESE PEOPLE DON'T UNDERSTAND YOU."

"GENUINE STRENGTH MAKES PEOPLE UNCOMFORTABLE, AND
THAT'S WHY THEY HATE YOU. BUT THAT'S WHY I LOVE YOU."

"I DON'T THINK YOU GOT TO WHERE YOU ARE BY BEING A 'BIRD-
BRAIN.' I THINK CLEAVER IS JUST TALKING OUT OF FRUSTRA-
TION."

"YOU EXPRESSED THAT PERFECTLY."

"'LET'S LOOK AT THE BOTTOM LINE,' YOU SAID? WAIT, LET ME WRITE THAT DOWN. 'LET'S LOOK AT THE BOTTOM LINE.' THAT'S FANTASTIC. THAT'S SO APROPOS."

"YOU REMIND ME SO VERY MUCH OF RONALD REAGAN."

"THIS IS OBVIOUSLY THE WORK OF A DISGRUNTLED EMPLOYEE WITH AN AX TO GRIND."

"SURE, BUNKER IS MANAGEMENT MATERIAL. HE'S GOT THAT DRINKING THING SQUARED AWAY, RIGHT?"

"I WOULDN'T WANT TO SEE HER URINE SAMPLE. OH, JUST A CASUAL REMARK."

"IT'S SAD THAT HUXTABLE BLAMES ME FOR HIS TROUBLES. BUT IT'S NOT HIS FAULT, REALLY—DRUGS TAKE A TERRIBLE TOLL ON PEOPLE."

"I DON'T KNOW...IF SOMEONE SNIFFS A LOT AND ACTS EXTREMELY NERVOUS DOES THAT MEAN ANYTHING?"

"SURE, HOULIHAN IS MANAGEMENT MATERIAL. SHE DID EXTRACT HERSELF FROM THAT CULT, RIGHT?"

"OH, YOU GIVE ME FAR TOO MUCH CREDIT."

"I'M SORRY, BUT I HAPPEN TO GENUINELY AGREE WITH YOU."

"NO, NOT ME...I DON'T HAVE ANY AMBITIONS LIKE THAT."

"IF I EVER AM FORTUNATE ENOUGH TO WIND UP RUNNING THIS BUSINESS, I WANT TO RUN IT JUST LIKE YOU."

"IF I EVER AM FORTUNATE ENOUGH TO HEAD THIS ORGANIZA-TION, YOU CAN BET I'M GOING TO FIND A SPECIAL PLACE FOR YOU."

PARTING SHOTS

Power corrupts, and absolute power is absolutely beautiful.

—Me

I have now given you all the ammo you're ever going to need to be a great leader.

I've taught you to dominate effortlessly, to oppress creatively, to make employees quail at your very presence.

I've taught you that a *miserable and confused* workforce is a *productive* workforce.

I've taught you how to take the grip of power and throttle inferiors with it.

I've taught you that terror is the shining key that unlocks the door to profit.

I've taught you that it's of no concern to you if your employees consider you a psychopath—*just as long as they do what you say.*

Most importantly, I've taught you that employees aren't actually people per se, but simply slaves to your will. They were put on this earth to do your bidding.

It is their *function* to serve you. That is why they are called *functionaries.*

Of course there are many warm, fuzzy PC types who refuse to acknowledge this basic fact of life.

Not you. You've got more sense. You know that your employees are tools. Tools to make your business grow. Tools to make you richer and more powerful than you ever dreamed possible.

So now it's time for you to *lock* and *load*. It's time for you to take it to the next step.

If you follow my lead, you'll find yourself blasting away to the very top of your organization.

If, however, after reading this book, you still maintain that these management techniques are too "tough" for you, too "regressive," a "violation" of the employer-employee relationship, or otherwise not to your liking, let me just say one final thing to you:

You're fired. You're fired from my book, and you're fired from my life. You'll never work in this town again.

How do you like that, weenie?

Now get out. And don't let the door hit you on the ass on the way out.

When the going gets tough, the tough go to minimum-security prison.
—Some Watergate schmuck who got caught

Postscript: A few weeks after I completed this manuscript, it appears that the crybabies and sore losers I mentioned at the beginning of this book have managed to get me indicted on a variety of trumped-up charges. Discrimination, harassment, wrongful termination, price-fixing, fraud—you name it, they got me on it. I'm not surprised. When the wimps can't play

BELOW-THE-BELT MANAGER

with the big boys, they *always* take them to court. That's okay. It ain't the first time at the dance for me.

Well, we'll just see who's got the bigger popgun. We'll see who's left standing after all the shots have been fired.

In the meantime, you go ahead and do as I say.

It worked for me.

T—
The best wishes
—Barb